HOW TO PRODUCE
SUCCESSFUL
ADVERTISING

Marketing in Action Series

Series Editor: Norman Hart

In producing this series, the advice and assistance has been sought of a prestigious editorial panel representing the principal professional bodies, trade associations and business schools.

The Series Editor for the Marketing in Action books is Norman Hart who is a writer of some ten books himself. He currently runs his own marketing consultancy, and is also an international lecturer on marketing and other such conferences as well as the leading business schools.

ALSO IN THIS SERIES

MARKETING IN ACTION SERIES

HOW TO PRODUCE SUCCESSFUL ADVERTISING

A Guide to Strategy, Planning and Targeting

Second Edition

A. D. FARBEY

KOGAN PAGE

The masculine pronoun has been used throughout this book. This stems from a desire to avoid ugly and cumbersome language, and no discrimination, prejudice or bias is intended.

First published in 1994
Second edition 1998

Kogan Page Limited
120 Pentonville Road
London N1 9JN

British Library Cataloguing in Publication Data

A CIP record for this book is available from the British Library.

ISBN 0 7494 2701 9

Typeset by Jean Cussons Typesetting, Diss, Norfolk
Printed and bound in Great Britain by
Biddles Ltd, Guildford and King's Lynn

Contents

Introduction

Many organisations now use advertising, for a wide variety of purposes. It has become a necessary tool of activity, and an increasing number of people are involved in either producing or commissioning advertising programmes. Large amounts of money are often spent.

It is clearly important to gain an effective result. This is achieved through efficient organisation of the advertising effort, the development of a practical action plan, and sensible control of how the money is spent. Success will come about with professionalism and practical expertise.

This book is aimed at those who will use advertising and who require insight into the day-to-day practice of producing advertisements and planning them skilfully. It does not dwell on the overlying theory. It sets out to provide a helpful working tool for new practitioners or those considering how best to begin on the road towards a successful advertising programme. The essence of this book is practicality – which is the essence, too, of advertising itself.

To J, M and E

1

What Advertising Can Do and How it Operates

WHY ADVERTISING?

Advertising today is a large enterprise. It is both an industry in itself and a tool used by a wide range of people. It represents a very considerable expenditure and so has to be approached carefully and efficiently. Advertising is widespread because it serves a purpose.

In a simpler society, or a smaller economy, or with a small population, relationships might be personal and direct, and there might be no need for anything other than personal dealing from individual to individual.

But, in a complex, large, industrialised society personal dealing needs to be supplemented and reinforced – by communication of an indirect kind and, among other things, by advertising. Advertising serves a contemporary purpose. It is a purpose dictated by scale, size, distance, convenience and cost. We advertise because it helps us if we do.

Advertising is not just a force for commercial organisations and large-scale industry, a tool of them and us. It is a method used across the length and breadth of society, for the following purposes:

■ for commercial business, to sell goods and services,
■ for recruitment, to obtain staff

- by central government, to inform the public
- by local authorities, to announce local services
- for books, or travel, or education courses
- for financial services or for entertainment
- by companies to announce their results or new ventures
- for health-care products or services
- by individuals, to buy and sell personal goods
- by political parties, to solicit votes.

The list of advertising usages extends much further. It is continuously widening. All these usages have a common denominator: the need to communicate a message, sometimes commercial, sometimes public service, sometimes for business, sometimes for private purposes.

Advertising communicates a message or proposition, which can contain or combine different purposes, of which two are the key characteristics:

1. advertising seeks to inform
2. advertising seeks to persuade.

The emphasis may vary. Pension-increase advertisements may inform more. Beer advertisements may persuade more. But in most advertisements there is the mixture of the two.

ITS PLACE IN THE MARKETING MIX

In the recent past, the concept of marketing, or rather of the market, has extended dramatically. The market is a potent idea, with wide meanings. Goods, services, commodities exist within markets and are subject to the laws of supply and demand. And central to the concept of the market is the idea of the customer. Goods, services, markets exist to supply and satisfy customers. That is the rationale of industry: to identify, obtain, supply and retain a customer.

The force that relates an organisation to its customers is the force of marketing. The marketing function is central to the whole task of servicing and retaining customers. And this seemingly simple idea has spread far out, from consumer goods, to services, to local authority operation, to financial institutions, to health-care and education. Most people are at one and the same time customers themselves, and professionally seeing to deal with customers in one way or another.

Along with the idea of the customer has grown the idea of the brand. Markets have grown from the commodity stage, selling generic or undifferentiated commodities (apples, oranges, gas stoves, houses) to the branded stage, selling separate, specific, unique, distinctive and individual concepts – the brand. The brand is not just a physical product. It has indeed a physical shape, but beyond that it has an image, a tradition, a general meaning for the customer. Soap powder means washing clothes. Persil means effectiveness, and reliability and care.

The idea of the brand has extended far, from consumer packaged goods to durables, to services, to industrial products and raw materials, to business products, to finance, to public authorities, to public utilities.

Persil is a brand. So are Massey-Ferguson tractors. Or IBM computers. Or Parcel Force delivery. Or the American Express Card. Or Job Centres.

It is true that in one sense the high-water mark of the brand concept may be receding. With the surge of retail multiples, own label and retail buying power, manufactured brands are sometimes on the defensive. But there, too, branding persists. Marks & Spencer is a retail brand with all the classic brand values associated with hitherto consumer products. Marks & Spencer is in itself a consumer product.

A key factor in this marketing process and in the development of brands is advertising. Or rather, marketing communications in general.

Organisations must build themselves around customers. The marketing function above all relates the organisation to the customer, as seen in Figure 1.1.

Figure 1.1 *The marketing function*

With a wide and dispersed customer base, there are two ways of reaching customers:

1. via an intermediary, or distributor
2. via the media of communication.

The link with the intermediary may be through a primary sales representative, but here too communication can be influential. Communication works throughout the process. This can be seen in Figure 1.2.

Figure 1.2 *The distribution chain*

Although it is particularly a key factor in the marketing process, communication can work in other spheres too:

■ *Marketing communication:* to help promote products, services and ideas and to help achieve commercial/business goals.
■ *Corporate communication:* to help inform about an organisation, so as to build up a strong relationship with its network of publics.

Most advertising expenditure springs from marketing needs. But an increasing volume reflects corporate or organisational communication purposes – local authority signs on building sites extolling the work of the council seem to be corporate communication in tone. Or is there a marketing intent here, too?

WHAT ADVERTISING CAN DO

Many advertisers want many things. Advertising is multi-faceted. To be effective, advertising programmes need to be specific in their goals, specific in their audiences and specific in their means.

Out of a myriad of effects, advertising can particularly help in the following areas:

■ *To create awareness:* it can help to make things known. On the whole, people do not deal with things they have never heard of, or they prefer not to.

■ *To create or develop favourable attitudes:* it can help to foster a positive view of the product or service.

■ *To develop a brand identity:* advertising can help invest a product with a special image or characteristic.

■ *To position a product in a market:* where a market is segmented, advertising can help position a product with a particular segment and identify with it. Rolls-Royce and Mini cars occupy different segments. Their communication reflects this and maximises this.

■ *To sustain relationships:* it is a force to build and strengthen producer–customer relationships over time.

■ *To persuade:* advertising puts up a case for the customer to be interested in the product on offer.

■ *To create demand:* Häagen Dazs or McDonald's. Communication makes the product seem desirable, worthwhile and attainable.

■ *To build up enquiries:* often advertising is a bridge between the product and a sales call. Its function is to obtain enquiries: for a sales call, or for literature, or for a sample, or for a price estimate.

■ *To support distributors:* where there is a distributive chain, the distributor may require reinforcement in the local marketplace. Advertising is one of the forces that can supply this.

■ *To sustain the organisation:* a company may need to consolidate, or re-establish, or explain or reposition or rebuild relationships. It wishes to strengthen old friends or build new ones. Here advertising may have a strong corporate role.

▦ *To launch new products:* advertising is a key weapon in the battery of services used to launch products into the marketplace.

▦ *To offset competition:* one characteristic of the recent past has been the growth of the market concept. Another is the growth of the brand. A third feature is the growth of competitive activity. As markets grow so usually does competition. Few markets remain monopolies. As the customer remains sovereign, and a multiplicity of suppliers arise to serve him or her, so competitive activity accelerates.

A prime example of this is telecommunications. From a simple monopoly producer with a short range of products has emerged a spread of suppliers and a cornucopia of services. Competition is the norm.

Advertising helps meet competitors and match competitors, by persuading the customer or providing a counter-claim. In an increasingly competitive world, suppliers must advertise to protect themselves against primary competition, and sometimes against other categories of product too.

▦ *To help provide a point of difference:* people do not favour 'me-too' products. The brand needs a difference, a unique personality, a point of interest, a feature which will isolate it from a multitude of others. Brands sell differences, or 'product pluses'. These can be powerfully conveyed through advertising. Guinness is not a brown stout: it is a unique, mystical beverage. Martini is not just another vermouth: it is a sophisticated, superior substance in its own right. Differences are of emotion, or style, or status as well as of product specification.

▦ *To help reach people:* in some cases, an organisation may need to reach an important contact group, but finds it cannot do so directly, not effectively or economically. But it may do so with advertising.

WHAT ADVERTISING CAN'T DO

It is, however, important not to overclaim for advertising. Potential advertisers may overpromise and expect rapid results and be disappointed when advertising cannot deliver this.

It is not a solve-all or universal fix-it for all business problems. The essence of advertising is that it delivers messages to audiences. There are limits to what messages can achieve.

Advertising ultimately is only as strong as the product or service it advertises. On the whole, an old advertising adage is correct: that you can sell someone a poor product once but not twice if the product fails to perform adequately. Advertising has a powerful but limited competence.

Advertising helps problem solving. But there are some problems it cannot solve and there are, indeed, some situations where it is wiser not to advertise at all.

When labour relations are poor, or the company is under-capitalised, or when its research and development programme has failed or when its pricing is inadequate, or when its financial controls have failed, then a corporate campaign extolling the virtues of the company will lack credibility. You cannot advertise your way out of corporate failure. When the product is obsolete, its quality low, its features irrelevant to the market, or its specification of little value to customers, advertising cannot rescue it. You cannot advertise your way out of product failure. All advertising can do is to buy a little time.

If the product is not available, if the customer is unable to obtain it, if it has no backing from the distributor, if there is a breakdown of supply, advertising it may only inflame the situation. You cannot advertise your way out of distribution failure.

Advertising is indeed part of a wider marketing or corporate process. It is part of a chain of activities, where the links are mutually dependent and where each link is only as strong as the weakest link in the chain. Advertising cannot overcome poor price, poor quality, poor distribution or poor organisation.

It cannot create demand when other elements have failed. It also cannot create demand when markets are low or do not exist in the first place. The public will remain indifferent. It is one of the factors that may help create a market, but markets are wider considerations, composed of a multitude of factors. Advertising can help *stimulate* a market, but this is usually a market that already has some being or some latent potential.

In general, advertising cannot produce results when market circumstances are poor and the other marketing elements are not functioning.

It has a more humble role to play than some of its more enthusiastic exponents would have us believe. It can only communicate what is possible to communicate.

CATEGORIES OF ADVERTISING

While there are infinite graduations of advertising, on the whole the bulk of advertising volume falls into fairly distinctive headings:

▪ consumer goods and services
▪ business-to-business goods and services
▪ public sector, central and local government
▪ recruitment
▪ financial
▪ personal and classified
▪ direct marketing.

Advertising campaigns also work on geographical scales:

▪ national or international
▪ local or regional.

However, while these groupings may have their own emphases, or disciplines and methods, there is a basic similarity between them in terms of the essential techniques. Communication has a strong set of common denominators.

HOW ADVERTISING WORKS

The bulk of this book sets out the essentials for conducting an advertising campaign. But successful advertising fundamentally springs from three crucial ingredients:

1. defining or identifying a target audience
2. finding advertising media which will reach that audience, and buying space
3. filling that space with a message to the audience – that is, writing, designing and producing the message, and then delivering it.

So, ultimately, in its basic form, advertising comprises:

▪ buying and selling media space
▪ developing and producing messages.

Commonly, there are a number of ways in which this may be carried out.

■ The advertiser may do it himself. Many do.
■ The advertiser may use a specialist service to take over the complete task – the advertising agency. Just as organisations use specialists in other areas of activity, so a professional service may be of benefit here.
■ The advertiser may use a specialist service just to plan and purchase media – a media independent, or media consultancy. Other ways would then be found of producing the messages.

THE PARTIES TO ADVERTISING

There are a multiplicity of participants in an advertising campaign – essentially it is a collaborative process. But there are three key levels.

1. *The advertiser*, who commissions advertising, controls it, uses it and pays for it.
2. *The advertising agency, or media independent*, which provides a specialist consultancy and planning service and which implements the programme once the client has authorised it.
3. *The media*, who provide the space or time, and who enable the process of communication to take place.

The process is a three-sided triangle, yet many-layered.

Behind the three main players lie a range of suppliers of those many specialised services without which advertising implementation cannot take place, such as:

■ press production, artwork, photography
■ TV production, filming, recording, writing music, animating
■ radio production, recording
■ exhibition design, stand fitting, transportation and servicing
■ direct mail planning, production, fulfilment, mailing
■ printing, literature production
■ research into advertising effectiveness.

This list can be illustrated in Figure 1.3.

Figure 1.3 *The communications triangle*

THE MEDIA PARTNERS

Advertising is sometimes called a partnership, although some partners are more equal than others. The media play a key role. We will be describing them in detail later, but for the moment it is helpful to indicate the vast range of media opportunities that can assist the advertiser, such as:

■ newspapers and magazines
■ TV
■ outdoor: posters and transport sites
■ radio
■ cinema
■ exhibitions
■ direct mail
■ telemarketing and the use of the telephone
■ new electronic media such as the Internet.

There are many smaller media beyond these. They provide the space, the instrument for the advertiser; they enable the advertising process to take place.

And it is the media which receive the bulk of the expenditures. Advertising is, in many senses, an investment: in the power and effect of media space and media communication. The strengths of the media are the strengths of the advertising campaign.

2

Setting Objectives and Developing a Strategy

ALWAYS SET AN OBJECTIVE

The advertising campaign is produced to achieve an aim, to achieve what the advertiser desires, or needs.

Advertising succeeds if it meets its requirements. It fails if it does not do so. The problem is that there is considerable room for misunderstanding or disagreement. One person may contend that the advertising looks good, says the right thing and has been a great help. Someone else in the organisation maintains that the advertising was irrelevant, did not mean anything and was a waste of time. Both probably work from different assumptions. They look for different things.

Advertising does not work in the abstract. It sets out to meet a concrete need, with a specific response. As an example, Guinness was developing a down-market image and was being eroded by brighter, lighter drinks. It needed a counter-claim. Hence, 'Guinness Is Genius', conveyed via bright, provocative and modern images. A positioning objective, met by a positioning response. Specific aims, specific programme.

Indeed, the more specific the advertising objective, the more helpful and the more specific can be the campaign development. That is to say, advertising – like most commercial processes – works by being *precise*. The more precise, the more effective.

Targeting must be precise, media selection must be precise, creative thinking must be precise and all have to spring from a precise statement of objectives. The function of the advertiser, the moment the time has come to consider an advertising programme, begins with the establishment of objectives. All else springs from this.

The question of course is, who exactly sets these objectives? There is room for confusion. An objective always must be set. But it can originate from a number of sources:

■ the person in charge of the advertising: the advertising manager, or product manager, or communications manager
■ the marketing director, in charge of the complete marketing effect
■ the corporate management: the department director, or the corporate chairman, or the board
■ another department which needs to use the advertising for its own purpose, eg the sales force
■ the advertising consultant or service, such as the advertising agency.

Objectives may proceed from a mix of all five, but on the whole it is wise for the communications manager to act both as an originator and a coordinator.

That is, he or she consults any other department concerned (such as sales), checks back with and takes advice from the management level, formulates a statement of objectives, then checks it back again with the management and obtains formal approval. This process is illustrated in Figure 2.1.

The communications manager is the communications professional and has the communications responsibility – and therefore

Figure 2.1 *Communications consultation process*

rightly should formulate the marketing need into communications terms. The sales force is allowed to put their point of view forward and the finance department is consulted on the financial and costing aspects.

The managing director needs both to state what is required from the management level, and to give approval to the final proposed statement of objectives. The advertising agency (if one is used) is informed about the objectives, may be asked an opinion but in the end has to act under the organisation's instructions – and does not have the ultimate responsibility for setting objectives. Many would not wish to do so.

In smaller organisations, a single person may at one and the same time combine both the management and communications roles. And in large organisations, a department director (eg marketing director) may assume the management role. But common to all is the one single priority: to set a clear, accurate, sensible and practical set of objectives, with everyone in agreement.

It should also be said that objectives can take two forms:

■ the simple, and informal, where one individual may quickly brief another, perhaps verbally and without complication
■ the formal, the written and the detailed.

The former is no doubt satisfactory for smaller campaigns, or incidental one-off advertisements. But for anything requiring considerable expenditures, on which major outcomes rely, there is no substitute for a detailed, formal statement, usually in written form.

MARKETING VERSUS COMMUNICATIONS

A common source of difficulty or inaccuracy is the very easy confusion between two kinds of objective:

■ marketing
■ communications.

If the chairman says to the advertising manager, 'Our sales are down. Go out and do me a £20,000 advertising campaign to sell 10,000 more units by early summer', this is likely to lead to confusion between the two kinds.

Marketing or corporate objectives specify what the whole organisation is setting out to do, often expressed in commercial terms:

■ to sell X amount of goods
■ to achieve Y amount of turnover or income
■ to gain Z percentage share of the market.

These are not in themselves communication goals. They are wider than that.

Communications or advertising objectives set out to state what the advertising is required to do in its own terms, which is usually a particular kind of effect on a selected target audience, such as:

■ to create awareness
■ to build demand
■ to create a favourable opinion.

It does not of itself sell goods (unless the subject area is direct marketing) but it creates the conditions for selling goods, as seen in Figure 2.2.

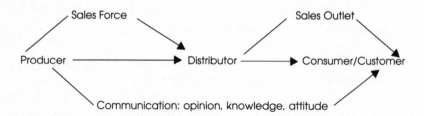

Figure 2.2 *The position of communications in the sales chain*

Therefore, the advertiser must be aware of the distinction between these categories of objective, and resist being saddled with objectives that do not properly lie in the advertising area, and so cannot properly be met.

TIMESCALE

Again, advertising works over time. The timescale is crucial. Many organisations work both by long-term and short-term objectives.

In many, short term is equated with the current financial year or even perhaps just one limited sales force journey cycle.

Here, too, it is necessary to be clear about objectives. An example of appropriate objectives might be:

▓ *short term:* to obtain a high awareness and recognition of the product
▓ *long term:* to have the product regarded as the best quality in the market, and to make it perceived as being more satisfying than any other.

Some advertising can only work over time; other results may be achieved more quickly.

Moral: set *specific* objectives, rooted in communications effects, and which can be practically achieved in a given campaign from financial year to financial year.

TYPES OF OBJECTIVE

Advertising aims to meet a need. The cardinal requirement at the outset, therefore, is to define what that need is: to identify it and make it specific.

In many instances, advertising is a tool for problem solving, in which case setting objectives becomes an exercise in evaluating what the problem really is. Solutions are only as strong as the problem evaluation.

In the next financial year, where do the problems lie? Is it a matter of:

▓ low awareness of the product, or its name or its specification?
▓ poor understanding of its features and its benefits, hostile or indifferent attitudes to it?
▓ confusion between the product and its competitors?
▓ weaknesses in certain sectors of the market, such as one worse performing region or weaker category of customer? or
▓ good awareness, but low actual use of the product?

Obviously, there is a world of difference between one campaign and another when the problems considered may lie so far apart.

Therefore, the advertiser must immediately conduct a complete evaluation of the stated problem, or an analysis of the situation where the problem is not stated. Sources of information or inspiration are varied:

■ analysis of sales data, broken down into constituent elements
■ analysis of data over time, and trend lines
■ analysis of the market, current movements and future directions
■ discussion with the sales force
■ discussion with distributors
■ discussion with representative customers
■ examination of the customer database
■ analysis of any information on customer attitudes
■ estimates of market shares and market share movements
■ evaluation of competition and competitive activity
■ scrutiny of competitive claims and any competitive advertising
■ possible research, tracking or attitude studies.

From these a variety of tactical responses may be required, depending on the problem which is identified, so that a relevant objective will emerge.

Types of objective are very varied:

■ *awareness:* people usually do not buy what they do not know
■ *recall:* that is, clear recall of product, brand name, specification etc
■ *attitude:* obtaining a favourable attitude
■ *attitude movement:* developing an attitude over time, and moving negative attitudes to positive
■ *product identity:* achieving a clear identity within the market
■ *product positioning:* setting the product within its market segment or giving it a particular place of its own
■ *benefits:* establishing what the product or service has to offer
■ *a product plus, or product differentiation:* sealing the product off from its competition, by giving it an advantage or a difference or a superior value against the others
■ *goodwill:* making the advertiser liked
■ *leading to a trial:* inducing the respondent to try the product out
■ *leading to a sales contact:* trying to get the respondent into contact with the organisation, and paving the way for a sales call
■ *enquiry for information:* an enquiry for a brochure, or product details

■ *penetration:* just getting *more*! That is, more respondents, more enquirers, more sales leads; in other words, increasing penetration into the market
■ *distributor support:* to reinforce the activities of the dealer, distributor or sales intermediary where the emphasis of the marketing is upon helping a distribution system which carries the burden of selling.

Each of the above is a particular objective, separate and specific. It should also be stressed that the fewer the objectives that are set, the better it is for the outcome. Campaigns that carry too unwieldy a load of objectives will stagger from one unrealistic expectation to another.

THE BRIEF

The advertising objectives that emerge may now be formed into a 'brief', which the advertiser can use for internal purposes, or which can be transmitted to outside advertisers, such as advertising agencies, for action.

The format for a brief will vary; no two are alike. But a short simple structure could well take the form of that in Figure 2.3.

ADVERTISING REQUIREMENT

Product/service _____

Period _____

Current sales position:

Current sales strengths:

Current sales weaknesses:

Present share of market and comparison with 12 months ago:

Customer profile:

Customer awareness levels:

What customers know:

What we want customers to know:

Advertising aim for the period:

    – customer objective

    – distributor objective

Level of enquiries needed:

Figure 2.3 *Advertising brief*

THE NEXT STEP – A STRATEGY

Many advertising situations do not have a complex or lengthy outcome. A Christmas greetings advertisement hardly warrants immense consideration. But an important need, with a formal set of objectives, does justify time and effort in order to develop an appropriate solution.

The question here is, how? That is, how is the objective to be achieved? How can the problem be overcome? How can the customer best be attracted? How can the product most effectively be offered?

The result of the how is the establishment of a strategy. The advertiser is the owner or the author of advertising strategy. Many people may be involved in the implementation of the strategy, or the execution of different tasks, but the formulation of the overall strategy is central to the whole advertising effort.

In essence, a strategy lays down the overall policy (briefly stated) for achieving the objective. It declares what the key features should be: that is, the key features for action, for what needs to be done.

For example, advertiser Jones requires new computer field staff, in a competitive market, where there are few people and many potential employers.

Strategy: stress the superior training benefits for the company and attract people to an open day to demonstrate this. Go to association member lists, and reach people at home via direct mail and telephone.

Advertiser Smith operates a Mediterranean holiday brochure. The market is depressed, there is intense competition, little differentiation between brochures and some consumer confusion.

Strategy: stress the superior price benefits and the availability of flights from local airports. Aim at the mid-market. Concentrate and dominate in the *Daily Mail* and *Daily Express*.

Advertiser Brown: a sixth-form college offering 'A' Level resits, with a fall in the market, a decline in the market-base, a large number of contenders, little knowledge among parents or students about alternative colleges and some confusion over examination results.

Strategy: feature the 'A' Level and GCSE results of last year. Show the record in improving examination grades. Stress the small size of classes. Build up enquiries for the prospectus. Use local press and mailings to other schools.

That is, *the strategy encapsulates the policy*, in terms of:

■ how the product or service is positioned
■ what benefits or attributes are featured
■ what the target audience is to be
■ how the message is best to be delivered.

The strategy meets the objective set through making the product or service as attractive to the target audience as possible, within the particular terms of the problem or task to be overcome.

A STRATEGY KIT

What tools does the advertiser have for formulating such a strategy? A simple set of ideas can point the advertiser in the right direction. Basic strategy decisions answer the following questions:

■ *Who is the target audience?* Who uses, purchases, decides? Where is the audience?
■ *What is the problem?* What area of weakness needs to be overcome?
■ *What does the customer want?* Taking the perceived area of weakness, what does the customer look for? What attributes, what qualities or values, what type of performance? What motivates the audience most?
■ *What does the product or service possess?* What are the tangible assets? What does the product do? What are its merits? Where are its deficiencies?
■ *How does it compare with the competition?* What are the advantages and disadvantages, the strengths or the weaknesses, against the competition?
■ *What is the principal asset or benefit?* What can be offered now? Or what could be offered in the future?
■ *How well does this benefit meet customer requirements?* Does the offer or promise meet the need? As well or better than competitors?
■ *What is the best means of delivering this promise?* The best physical means. Media type or communications type.

Given an area or region, a timescale and a budget, a strategy will evolve. The more detailed communications plan will then establish the best method or means of activity to communicate this strategy to the target audience.

A STRATEGY CHECKLIST

◼ Is this a new product or an established one?
◼ What does it *do*, precisely?
◼ What are its main features and benefits?

Features	*Benefit of each feature*

◼ How does this compare with the market?

Product/service feature	*Competitor (a)*	*Competitor (b)*

◼ How do the prices compare?
◼ Who is the target audience?
   – user/buyer/decision maker?
   – by size/by category?
◼ What do they want from the product/service category?

Requirements

◼ How do they now assess the product in terms of these criteria?

Requirements	*Audience rating*

◼ What are the present sales weaknesses?
◼ What are the present sales opportunities?
◼ What are the present levels of awareness:
   – of the product?
   – of the category?
◼ What is the central benefit which can now be offered?
◼ How best can awareness be improved?

3

How to Select your Target

GET THE TARGET RIGHT

One of the main questions in advertising is: who? Who do you sell to, who do you persuade, who is the key influence, who actually purchases, who makes the key decisions, who is most important to you, who – in short – is your audience?

Advertising costs money. Often the sums are considerable and rarely does the money come easy to the advertiser. That money should be spent properly, which means it should be spent accurately. A failure of efficiency is a waste of the budget.

And efficiency means directing the right messages in the right way at the right people. Advertising equals communication. It is vital for effective communication to address the correct audience – the one that matters.

Targeting lies at the heart of the communications process. Right at the very beginning of the process the advertiser must decide who to talk to, who to select as the audience for the message. Sometimes this is simple. An advertisement for a cook for a school canteen would begin by finding people with suitable experience – those who are or have been cooks in an industrial, educational or health-care kitchen. It is an obvious starting point.

An advertisement for dental chairs would aim at dentists (though maybe not only dentists. Targeting gets more complex quite rapidly).

An announcement about pension increases would go to the elderly.

A new Civic Centre in Wolverhampton would be announced to the people of Wolverhampton.

Advertising a new high-performance motorbike would no doubt aim at people interested in, possessing, or currently using a motorbike.

But targeting is not always as simple as that.

Who do you select as the target for a new Mini car? The young? Those with less money? Those who want a second car? Mums?

Who would be the target for sherry advertising? The elderly? Confirmed drinkers? Up-market households? Or new drinkers?

And who do you advertise to for office copiers? Think of the possibilities. Targets might include:

■ secretaries
■ department heads
■ purchasing managers
■ managing directors
■ all middle managers in a firm.

The answer is a matter of judgement.

Get it right and the campaign will strike home. Get it wrong, and the money is wasted, the opportunity is wasted, the time is wasted.

It is, commonsense dictates, vital to get the target right. Sometimes this is an easy matter, and sometimes the target is difficult to determine – sometimes, indeed, almost impossible to determine. Which is what makes advertising an art as well as a science.

WHO IS THE TARGET?

Different campaigns have different targets. Ethical pharmaceuticals, machine tools, agricultural fertilisers, swimwear, Heineken lager and the local bingo hall all have different, varying and specific target audiences.

What is common is the need to make audience selection *precise*.

That is the vital aspect of communications planning. The concept of precision. The more precise the targeting, the more effective the message will be, and the less wasteful the campaign.

Planning aims to become more and more precise: not all people but these people, not all house-owners but a type of house-owner, not all holiday-makers but a type of holiday-maker, not all motorists but a type of motorist.

Few products sell to universal audiences and are all things to all people. Most products have their own profile, their own particular type of customer, their own segment of the market, their own special character.

Indeed, the trend in marketing over the past decade has been to encourage this: to divide markets up and produce highly specific entries for specific segments. The trend, in short, has been towards 'niche marketing'.

You do not sell to everyone, but to *your* market. Separate it out. Consider the motorcar market again. It actually is at one and the same time a wide variety of dissimilar subsections: Rolls-Royce, Minis, estate cars, Land Rovers, sports cars, middle-sized cars for sales-people, two-seater cars and eight-seater 'People Movers'. Not a market, but markets.

To make matters worse, markets change and move. Types of customer will alter over time. Holidays in Florida were rare, they then became up-market, but more frequent, and have now become mass-market. Targets change. Advertisers must keep ahead of such change.

So, who indeed *is* the target? This will depend on whether the situation is commercial or non-commercial. In a commercial campaign, in order to achieve a sale the advertiser will have to consider three forces which may lead towards the sale:

1. Who uses the product?
2. Who actually purchases it?
3. Who decides to obtain it?

These are the classic three partners in the buying process: users, purchasers and decision makers. But there may also be a fourth one still – influencers! Taking the model of the office copier mentioned earlier:

■ the secretary may use it
■ the purchasing manager may issue the purchase order
■ the managing director or the senior directors may make the decision.

But around them may swarm nearly everyone in the organisation. All interested in, or with a view about, or making occasional use of, the office copying machines. They are influencers. They cannot help it.

Who *are* these users, purchasers and decision makers, in practice? That is, can they be identified, or specified? Or named?

Central to the targeting decision is the question of defining the target audience. That is, defining:

■ who it should be
■ where and who they are.

AUDIENCE DEFINITION

The simplest way to define an audience is to say – 'my customers'. But even at this simple level, two judgements are involved:

1. Who and what *are* these customers?
2. Should the audience be the present, existing customers or perhaps include past, lapsed customers, or why not new, potential customers?

It will all depend on the business objectives and the current state of trade. The definition may have to vary over time, in line with results and needs.

But it is necessary to describe these customers in a simple, universal way, which can be readily understood and which can be quickly translated into practical, realistic steps – such as media planning.

Audience definition *systems* are therefore necessary and are in wide use within advertisers and agencies.

The main split in definition systems is between consumer products and business-to-business products.

Demographic/Socio-economic

Audience definition systems endeavour to build up a model of the market and of the likely customer. The most prevalent system for many years has been that of socio-economic and demographic characteristics. My product may sell especially well to a particular section of the population or have a particular customer profile:

■ by sex (men or women)
■ by age group (younger, middle-aged, older)

■ by area (national, or weighted towards one particular area rather than another – few products, indeed, have an even spread nationally)
■ by socio-economic group.

This last category is a combination of income and 'class' or, at least, occupational group. The famous, and perhaps overfamiliar, way of characterising this is by letters:

■ A – upper
■ B – higher professional
■ C1 – lower professional
■ C2 – skilled non-professional
■ D – manual workers, unskilled labour
■ E – pensioners, low-waged, unemployed.

It should be noted that these categorisations do not stand still and are, indeed, in the process of being redrawn.

Most product categories *do* have something of this breakdown. The value of the classification is as a prediction of likely behaviour.

It is more likely that ABs will fly on Concorde. They have the money. It is more likely that C2D class young men will read *The Sun*. It is more likely that younger, more career-minded women will read *Cosmopolitan* magazine. It is more likely that the affluent retired will go on Caribbean cruises than those living on the state pension alone.

Indeed, many products have long used this system of definition and have found it fruitful. Its strength is that it can be physically established. And can be related readily to the profile of advertising media.

Its weakness, however, is that it is based on static social classification within a changing world and that it takes little account of the modes of thinking or the attitudes of a mobile society.

Geodemographic

This is a system for dividing the audience up by area, by type of residence, by the implied value of location.

The population can be split into location groups. Each is a kind of prediction of behaviour. Those living in large detached houses will very likely behave and purchase differently from those living on pre-war council estates.

Geodemographic targeting lends itself particularly well to direct marketing, to mailing and to localised media such as local press or posters.

Psychographic

What your customers may do relates not just to who they are, or where they live, or what they earn but also to what they think, what their attitudes are, how they relate to the world, what their behaviour pattern is. Markets may well be split by behaviour pattern as much as by income data. Behaviour is often defined as 'lifestyle'. Psychographic targeting seeks to model the market in terms of the lifestyle, attitudes and behaviour patterns of groups of individuals. These, too, can be likely predictors of purchase patterns.

Many current phrases, or well-oiled labels, are based upon previous psychographic analyses. For example:

■ Yuppies: younger, sociably mobile
■ Dinkies: double income couples without the cost of children.

These are generally sensible concepts, which can illuminate a market, if not overused. Their problem, however, is twofold:

1. There are no standard psychographic classifications. They vary from company to company or researcher to researcher.
2. They are sometimes fanciful, and difficult to put into practice.

But used with care – and a sense of humour – they can indeed throw light on target groups, and on potential customer behaviour.

Some examples

Socio-economic splits can be:

■ all adults
■ men
■ women
■ housewives
■ children
■ age groups:
  – below 15
  – 15–19
  – 20–24
  – 25–34

- 35–44
- 45–54
- 55–64
- 64+

■ social grade:
  - A – higher managerial, professional
  - B – intermediate managerial, administrative
  - C1 – supervisory, clerical, junior managerial
  - C2 – skilled manual workers
  - D – semi or unskilled manual workers
  - E – state pensioners, casual workers, unemployed

■ area:
  - by TV region
  - Registrar General region/standard region
  - Nielsen areas (sales research organisation)
  - county

■ household income, eg:
  - £25,000 +

■ life-stage groupings (BMRB)
  - 15–34 not married, no children
  - 15–34 married, no children
  - 15–34 married, with children
  - 35–54 with children
  - 35–54 no children
  - 55–64 not social grade E
  - age 65+ and social grade E

■ Sagacity groupings (lifecycle stages):
  - dependent
  - pre-family } better-off } white collar
  - family   } worse-off } blue collar
  - late

■ Acorn groups (geodemographic) with six categories and 17 groups, including:
  - agricultural areas
  - modern family higher income
  - older housing, intermediate status
  - older terraced housing
  - council estate (category 1, category 2, category 3)
  - mixed inner metropolitan areas
  - high-status non-family areas
  - affluent suburban housing
  - better-off retirement areas

■ Super Profiles lifestyle (example of psychographic/geodemo-graphic)
  - affluent achievers
  - thriving greys
  - settled suburbans
  - nest builders
  - urban venturers
  - country life
  - senior citizens
  - producers
  - hard-pressed families
  - have-nots
■ Mosaic classifications:
  - high-income families
  - blue collar owners
  - council flats
  - town houses/flats
  - independent elders
  - country dweller
  - suburban semis
  - low-use council
  - Victorian low status
  - stylish singles
  - mortgaged families
  - institutional areas

These are only *some* of the available current definitions from which two points emerge:

1. The importance of selecting a target definition system carefully.
2. The way in which targetings can be followed through: in media terms by such elements as mailing, or poster coverage, or use of local radio; and in the creative sphere, by tone of voice or type of message. Targeting is a matter of commonsense, consistency and persistence from which the whole advertising campaign will spring.

INTENSITY AND WEIGHTING

What has been described up to now has been categories. Taking a population and dividing it into categories: young, old, suburban, aspiring. The aim is to relate these categories to a value. That is, to the potential value of the customer. But these categories are very generalised. There may not necessarily be a particular sales value in them. So another method of targeting may indeed be to target by sales value, or by sales intensity.

A well-known concept in statistics is the Pareto effect – the 80:20 phenomenon. That is, not all customers are equal and the same. Some will buy more than others. In a sense, 80 per cent of my volume sales may be made by only 20 per cent of all my customers. Some people will not eat chocolate bars, some will eat them very seldom, some will eat them when they are in the mood and some people are chocaholics, devouring chocolate bars as soon as they are hungry. In others words, the product *category* and *my* product itself have:

■ non-users
■ light-users
■ medium-users
■ heavy-users.

The advertiser has an important decision to make. If not all customers are equal, who to advertise to? In a clear sense, it is a business decision:

■ Do you protect your heavy users?
■ Do you try to convert your lighter users into heavier users?
■ Do you try to bring in non-users?

Or do you do all three at one and the same time?

Weighting the advertising by intensity of purchase or usership is an investment decision. What type of expenditure will bring in the greatest return? This judgement is only realistic if there is a way of actually achieving this weighting in practice and of being able to relate usership to media selection.

There are a number of systems which do provide for this. The best known example is the Target Group Index, a large-scale research system which breaks down a wide range of product categories and products within those categories by intensity or frequency of use – heavy, medium and light. It then correlates the users and the media, such as:

■ heavy user – newspaper read

■ medium user – magazine read
■ light user – TV seen etc.

It is therefore possible to do two things:

1. To draw up a target profile by intensity of use, and then to draw up a media schedule which covers the target.
2. To allocate weightings for the advertising. Maybe the campaign should spend proportionately. Of a campaign spend of 100 per cent, maybe the media could be weighted pro rata to usership. For example: heavy users 80 per cent, medium and light users 20 per cent.

Money is going out in proportion to the value of the customer.

SUB-MARKETS

The previous concepts assume that the advertiser has one uniform market. But sometimes on closer examination the market turns out not to be the predicted market, but a variety of sub-markets.

A motorcar may sell to a range of customer types. For example:

■ private purchasers
■ fleet owners of company cars
■ car-hire operators
■ taxi drivers
■ the police.

So, in this case, there is not a market but a sequence of separate and differing markets.

Or take a brand of cold meat. It may sell to:

■ people at home
■ people in pubs
■ people in factory canteens.

Here there are three clear targets:

1. consumers
2. pub owners
3. industrial caterers.

Always remembering a fourth audience: the distributor, who should be kept informed, and influenced, and motivated.

It is therefore valuable to draw up a plan, or scheme, or model of the market. How is it composed? How does it break down? What is the value of its constituent elements?

The model may be informal, or it may be highly formalised, based on considerable evidence and examination. Here too it is necessary to ascribe weightings to each constituent and to give a value to them. So, for example, the media budget could be split as follows:

▓ the consumer market – 70 per cent of sales
▓ the pub market – 20 per cent of sales
▓ industrial caterers – 10 per cent of sales.

The result of this may be not one campaign but a set of separate, specialised campaigns each with its own target, its own sub-budget, its own media plan and its own messages – precisely geared to a precise market.

THE BUSINESS-TO-BUSINESS TARGET

The business-to-business target shares many of the characteristics of the targeting previously outlined:

▓ breaking down into sub-markets
▓ weighting to frequency of use
▓ weighting to value of customer.

Indeed, much business-to-business advertising does precisely that. It may divide the target audience down into value categories. One way is by period of purchasing:

▓ those who purchased recently
▓ those who purchased some while ago
▓ those who purchased a long while ago.

Messages and tactics will vary according to the category. Or alternatively by value of customer. Activities could be split by:

▓ larger customers

■ medium-sized customers
■ smaller customers.

Weighting and differential spend are a consequence of these definitions.

Another simple approach is to target by region. By sales region, or wholesaler region, or by area weight of purchasing, via an average:

■ average sales regions
■ above average regions
■ below average regions.

The key decision is whether to spend evenly, or to build up weaker regions, or to invest further in strong regions.

Here, too, media can be weighted and money spent in proportion.

At the heart of the campaign plan is the need to decide who counts most: the user, the buyer, or the decision maker? This is a critical decision. If you advertise, how can the advertising best achieve a sale? How will it work? Who best gives a return to the advertising pound spent?

One system often used in business-to-business communication is that of the 'decision-making unit' or DMU.

In real life, the decision is often made not by one person, but by a group of people. Overall, the advertising should get to decision makers. They count above all others. So, it is essential to examine the decision-making process in any particular market. And here again, a variety of sub-markets may emerge, each with its own decision-making structure.

Take a general market. It might perhaps break down into three sub-markets:

1. Sole traders. One simple target group. Usually smaller businesses;
2. Medium-sized companies with decisions by:
   – heads of user departments
   – the procurement division
   – the board of directors;
3. Specialised users, research based with decisions by:
   – R & D management
   – the R & D staff themselves

- the procurement division
- the finance director
- the board of directors;

from which three programmes may evidently be needed, each targeted, each specific. Business-to-business targeting therefore very much rests on the need to model the market, and to establish the values of business within it.

THE CORPORATE AUDIENCE

Advertising for corporate purposes will again have to define the target precisely. The audience for an organisation as a whole will be its public. Or rather, publics:

■ customers
■ consumers or users
■ staff
■ suppliers
■ the local community around the offices or factories
■ the finance community, bankers or institutions
■ shareholders, the City
■ those who may influence the company's progress, such as local authorities, or trade associations, or government
■ opinion formers, journalists, political leaders.

A corporate campaign should cover three basics:

1. What is the communications need?
2. Who matters most?
3. What degree of importance does each grouping have?

Here, too, the concept of categories and of grouping will be relevant. Targeting has a common philosophy.

TARGETING CHECKLIST

■ Who are the customers?
■ Where are they? By region, by locality?
■ How does the customer base break down:
  – by size?
  – by usage or performance or product type bought?
  – by frequency of use?
  – by frequency of purchase?
■ Who precisely uses the product?
■ Who purchases the product?
■ Who decided on the purchase?
■ What is the purchase-making process?
■ What is the decision-making process?
■ What type of customer is it:
  – by professional category? or
  – by age/sex/area/socio-economic grouping?
■ Can you describe the customer by:
  – type of behaviour?
  – attitude?
  – lifestyle?
■ Do you have one type of customer or several?
■ Does the market segment into constituent elements?
■ What is the value of each element?
■ Do these elements or sub-markets behave in different ways?
■ What are the trends in each sector?
■ How do you see them developing?
■ Do you have heavy, medium and light users?
■ Can you separate them?
■ Who are they? How do they differ?

4

How to Select Media

THE TASK

There is a multiplicity of advertising media in Britain. Selecting the right media for a particular job can sometimes be simple and a matter of routine and sometimes be difficult and shrouded in unknowns.

The key fact behind media planning and media selection is that this is the way in which the bulk of the advertising money is spent. The choice of media will determine how well that money is spent and how far the advertiser receives value. There is an enormous responsibility to plan effectively and to justify the choices made. The media plan represents a financial investment just as much as any other commercial expenditure and needs to be subject to the same disciplines as other similar investments. Media planning covers two stages:

1. planning, and developing an effective media selection
2. buying the media selected.

The present chapter deals with the former.

Media selection itself follows three main elements:

1. identifying those media which best reach the target audience
2. getting the optimum use out of them
3. ensuring that the budget is deployed to best advantage and that fullest value is obtained.

THE RANGE OF OPTIONS

Selection will depend on the product and its advertising requirements. The key question in media selection is: which are the most effective media in which to advertise this product at this time? It is, of course, necessary to define what is meant by 'the most effective'. Efficient advertising requires those advertising media which:

▧ can reach the target audience as completely as possible
▧ can deliver a message with maximum visibility
▧ can deliver messages economically, and within the budget set
▧ can communicate within an environment which is suitable to the product and its audience.

One of the features of media selection for many products (perhaps not all, some impose their own limitations) is that there is a wide range of possible media available. Indeed, the quantity of potential media has extended rapidly over the last few years. We have been living through a period of intensive media expansion, and looking to the future it is probable that the proliferation of media will continue, both nationally and internationally.

Selecting media is, therefore, a matter of considering the range of options available, and deciding which offer the most effective possibilities. It is, indeed, a process of elimination. There are a number of key stages in this process:

1. developing a brief, and setting the objectives for the media
2. examining the options and then developing an overall media plan which can meet the objectives
3. agreeing the media shortlist
4. developing a final schedule of those media to be used
5. purchasing the necessary space or time
6. checking that the advertising has actually appeared, and then evaluating what audience size it has delivered
7. paying for the space and time.

The present chapter will deal with the planning aspects and the next chapter will cover the process of media purchasing.

At the centre of planning is the vital question of examining the various options available and comparing the relative merits of each. The task is to reach an audience. There are, in general terms, two main groups of media which can be used:

1. advertisement space available in the wider media of communications, those produced to inform or entertain the public
2. media which are purely a form of advertising in themselves.

These are often classified as 'above and below the line' – a term originally borrowed from the terminology of government statistics and accountancy.

Another way of grouping them is again as two main groups:

1. messages delivered via the other media of communications
2. messages which are delivered direct from the originator to the audience.

The main categories of advertising media now available to the advertiser are the following:

1. press or print media. These have two main sub-categories:
   - press and newspapers
   - magazines
2. television, in a variety of forms
3. outdoor – posters or transportation advertising
4. radio
5. cinema.

Direct forms of delivering messages include:

6. exhibitions
7. direct mail, ie mailing the message
8. telemarketing, ie telephoning the message.

Another category which is much used, and which is separate from the press category of newspapers and magazines, is:

9. directories.

There has also been a considerable growth in electronic systems:

10. Internet
11. videos and CD-ROM
12. fax.

These are, as yet, comparatively small but are bound to grow.

Each of these categories has its own characteristics, structure, method of operation and cost factor.

Within the general *category* there may then exist a multitude of actual *media*. Directories are a category. Within that, there are over 5000 different directories, ranging widely in size, type and cost.

Thus there are two levels of option which the advertiser must consider:

1. a choice between competing categories of media
2. a choice of individual candidate media within those categories.

The choice may be relatively restricted and obvious, or there may be a large and widening list of media which will take time and effort to consider.

THE MEDIA BRIEF

The advertiser has a number of facilities for the selection and placement of media space:

■ they can do it themselves, or within their organisation
■ the use of an advertising agency
■ the use of a media independent.

Before the development of a media plan, it is helpful to set out a final and fully considered brief for the media. A brief is vital when using an advertising agency or media independent, but is useful even if the advertiser is producing the plan directly as it clarifies what is required and ensures that the eventual media plan is as accurate as possible.

On many occasions, an advertisement may be immediate, or simple, or one-off, or casual or of low priority. In which case, a formal media brief may not be required and would be a waste of time. If the organisation places an insertion in the annual trade ball, or runs a Christmas greetings advertisement in the trade press, or puts up a roadway sign pointing towards the factory, a fully-fledged media brief is hardly appropriate. But when the advertising has a heavy budget, or is ongoing, or has a serious purpose, or has a major task to achieve, then the production of a media brief is desirable – and may be inevitable.

MEDIA BRIEF

Company_____

Product_____

Date_____

(1) Target audience/audiences

(2) Area

(3) Timing and duration of campaign

(4) Purpose of campaign

(5) Media needs

(6) Creative considerations

(7) Budget

Figure 4.1 *An example of a media brief*

There are two types of media brief:

1. quick, informal and perhaps verbal: just a short instruction to an advertising agency, leaving it to the agency to form its own conclusions
2. a formal, developed, written document – in memorandum or letter form.

The latter is preferable, and certainly it is sensible to put all instructions into writing if only to save arguments later or to avoid differing interpretations of what was asked for.

The brief sets out the main elements of the media requirement, as seen in Figure 4.1.

Target audience
This should stipulate the precise target for the advertising:

■ on a consumer/direct customer level
■ on a trade or intermediary level.

Area
National, regional or local.

Timing
How long the advertising should run. Key buying days may be suggested.

Purpose of campaign
Differing purposes may lead to differing media choices, so that it is important to clarify what the purpose may be.

It may be to recruit three senior managers, and also to indicate to the industry that the company is now progressing fast. In this case, the media must reach potential applicants but also reach the wider industry.

It may be to achieve high recall of the product features and high awareness of the product name. In this case, the media must be intrusive and have high impact.

It may be to build strong consumer awareness and convince the distributor of our support for the product. In this case, the media used must be those perceived as important by the distributor, as well as those with good coverage of the consumer.

Media needs
The advertiser can state a preference for:

■ wide coverage
■ a high degree of repetition
■ very precise targeting, with little wastage, etc.

Creative considerations
Here a variety of needs can be expressed. For example:

■ colour presentation of the product
■ product demonstration
■ a coupon or a telephone number, to encourage enquiries
■ a lengthy message (as with pharmaceuticals)
■ a map or diagram
■ a strong brand name registration.

Budget
It may be argued that the brief should lead to the budget and that the advertising agency should be free to suggest what is best and therefore how much it should cost. But, in practice, the advertising budget is part of the wider question of company finance and control, and usually is subject to what the company

sees as affordable. It therefore tends to set out a budget at the beginning, rather than leaving this open. The company can only spend what it knows it has in the bank.

Having published the brief, an advertiser may debate it with the advertising agency and may allow it to be modified or rewritten, if they can be persuaded that there are good grounds for doing so.

After all, advertising is a collaborative effort. But, ultimately, the responsibility and ownership of a media brief is an advertiser's. Because the *advertising* belongs to them.

Once the brief is agreed, the different options can be formulated.

THE MEDIA CATEGORIES AND THEIR CHARACTERISTICS

We will take the main media categories separately, and itemise their principal features and benefits.

It may help to set the media into context by establishing their scale and relative size.

In terms of display advertising, various organisations or sources monitor annual media category turnover, such as the Advertising Association and the *Advertising Statistics Yearbook*.

There have been fluctuations of turnover between media types, and relative short-term movements, but over a 25-year period the following rankings have emerged:

■ Press is still the largest category.
■ TV is second. It has grown from around 60 per cent of the size of press to around 90 per cent. It might conceivably overtake press as the largest advertising medium but still has a way to go.
■ Direct mail is the third largest medium and has trebled in size over the past 15 years.
■ Directories as a separate category are the fourth largest, and have grown sixfold over the last 15 years.
■ Next follows outdoor and transportation, relatively static in the immediate past.
■ Radio has grown rapidly. It still has only some 60 per cent of the size of outdoor, but is forecast to grow, and to expand substantially.
■ Cinema is smallest in ranking, but has recovered from a low in the 1970s and early 1980s, to make solid progress later on.

■ Data for telemarketing are doubtful, due to the difficulty of splitting commercial calls from private calls – but it is undoubtedly now one of the major growth sectors.
■ The money spent on Internet advertising is still much smaller than for the main media, but it is growing rapidly.

Press

The press medium breaks down into two major sections: newspaper and magazine. These in turn divide into a variety of specific subsections, each with its own distinctive character and advertisement benefits. Among newspapers there are:

■ national daily newspapers
■ national Sunday newspapers
■ regional morning newspapers
■ regional evening newspapers
■ regional Sunday newspapers
■ regional weekly newspapers.

Among magazines there are:

■ general interest consumer magazines
■ special interest consumer magazines
■ business-to-business/professional magazines
■ trade magazines.

When confronted with a need, the advertiser can gain varying benefits from each of these sections, and can match the choice to the need.

National daily newspapers
These can provide the advertiser with a flexible choice. The national daily press offers:

■ high circulations
■ a range of titles, each with its own specific audience profile, allowing precise targeting of audience types
■ intensity of readership (ie it is read closely)
■ a variety of sections (eg educational, travel, situations vacant) which again assist audience targeting.

National Sunday newspapers
These have a similar character to the daily press but:

■ offer larger readerships
■ offer a lengthier period of reading.

To oversimplify, the daily press possesses greater news value but the Sunday press has a longer life in the home and may be read over Sunday and the early weekdays.

Regional morning newspapers
These offer the advertiser the news value of the national press with a closer and deeper relationship of local items. But there are comparatively few major cities with their own *morning* newspapers (such as the *Birmingham Post*). Much of this ground has been surrendered to the nationals.

Regional evening newspapers
This is a substantial section. A large number of towns and cities possess a local evening newspaper, which presents its readers with high news value and strong local content. Many of these (eg the *Manchester Evening News* and the *Yorkshire Evening Post* (Leeds)) have major circulations and are local institutions. They offer:

■ the ability to target a particular city or region
■ the opportunity to support local distributors
■ a close readership
■ news value.

They are a primary medium for local business, for local government and for the local retail trade.

Regional Sunday newspapers
While regional Sundays operate in only a few English cities (eg Newcastle) they have a strong position in Scotland, where two titles in particular – *The Mail* and *The Post* – have a proportionately massive coverage of the local population. In which case they combine the local strength of the regional evening with the depth and length of readership of the Sunday press.

Regional weekly newspapers
These form the bulk of the regional press. Weeklies cover most

towns and cities, with many towns running two or more weeklies, and with a large number of titles covering county or part-county areas. As a result, virtually all areas of Britain, big or small, have at least one local newspaper. Regional weeklies offer:

▪ the ability to go very local in scale
▪ a sound readership
▪ high coverage of local homes, with length of life in the home.

Again, they are the core medium for local advertisers: for local retail, motorcar, estate agency and local authority advertisers, among many others. They offer the national advertiser the ability to support local distributors, or to operate localised promotions.

General interest consumer magazines

While Britain has a limited number of large circulation general magazines (of which a fair example is the *Reader's Digest*) there is one type which does offer enormous size: the insert magazines produced with national newspapers on a Saturday or Sunday. These have a similar circulation to the parent newspaper. They provide the benefits of colour, large readerships and length of life, but can be proportionately expensive for the advertiser, with uncertain actual reading.

Special interest consumer magazines

There is a multiplicity of magazines aimed at special consumer interests. One large example is that of TV programme magazines (eg *Radio Times*). Circulations vary from the huge to the limited and cover virtually every consumer interest or spare-time activity, from sports, to gardening, to motoring, to food and drink, to videos and home entertainment.

The benefit for the advertiser is the obvious one of being able to match the specialist product or audience to a particular magazine, precisely, with little waste within the right editorial environment.

Women's magazines

This is so large a section of magazine titles that it is usually regarded as a section unto itself. Titles range from the general (*Marie Claire*) to the specialist (*Good Housekeeping*). Women's magazines fall into two groups:

1. weekly magazines (such as *Woman's Own*). Circulations here have been generally flat
2. monthly magazines (such as *Cosmopolitan*), a growth sector over the past 20 years, with a wide variety of new titles.

Women's magazines allow the advertiser to target the various audiences of women who are responsible for a high proportion of consumer spending. Specific editorial appeal can match the product to the audience. Across sub-groups, such as teenagers, early 20s, young working women, home-makers, the older woman etc.

Readership is intense and length of life considerable for each issue.

Men's magazines
This was traditionally a smaller category, but has grown substantially, especially among younger men. Some titles now have considerable circulation (such as *FHM* or *GQ*).

Here again, this category offers a strong opportunity for targeting.

Business to business
The UK possesses an enormous proliferation of business-to-business, technical, industrial and professional magazines which cover the vast majority of particular business or professional areas. Some industries are covered by a wide range of specific and varying titles. For example, most individual medical specialities are covered, while there are now over a hundred magazines devoted to the computer industry.

The benefit to the advertiser for those particular market groups is obvious and important. For many advertisers this is a core medium, offering them the benefits of:

■ selective and targeted readership
■ a strong fit between product and marketplace
■ close attention and readership from issue to issue
■ little wastage
■ appropriate surrounding editorial.

This category is for these reasons often the first media choice.

Trade magazines

These cover particular distributive or industrial trades, eg *The Grocer*, or *Builders Merchants' Journal*. Again they offer the value of a targeted audience, often with a high and important purchasing power.

Television

The television set is becoming a primary information source in the home, rather than just a purveyor of television programmes. Indeed, the telecommunications sector is likely to be the key growth area across the whole of the economy. There is now a wide range of services offering advertisement time:

■ terrestrial television: the traditional TV channels, comprising ITV (Channel 3), Channel 4 and Channel 5. That is, there are now three commercial channels to two BBC non-commercial channels
■ cable TV, with a large number of homes capable of choosing from a range of cable programmes
■ satellite, with a multi-provision of programmes
■ video, itself a form capable of carrying commercials
■ teletext (Ceefax, Oracle), which is both a form of information and an advertising form.

To date, the bulk of advertising goes into terrestrial TV, but the newer forms now offer an alternative and a competition as they grow in audience and in programme availability.

Satellite already has a wide base of homes capable of receiving terrestrial TV and a steadily growing audience. The majority of households are cabled and capable of cable TV installation.

Terrestrial TV is the preferred medium for many national advertisers because it has impact, high visibility, the power to demonstrate, the power to tell a story. It uses colour, sound, movement, music.

But TV has a more characteristic benefit than that:

■ audience can be selected by programme type or time of day
■ TV is a regional medium, and can provide area coverage
■ it has facilities for the local advertiser
■ it is effective for test-marketing or product launches.

In addition to spot advertising, there has been the growth in sponsorship of programmes.

But, for many advertisers, terrestrial TV is a difficult medium to consider because:

■ TV time is expensive – TV is perhaps the most expensive medium proportionately
■ the cost of TV production also is high
■ audience size is static and audiences are becoming fragmented.

Here, Channels 4 and 5 may be more usable for the smaller budget than ITV (Channel 3).

Alternatively, satellite and cable may also offer the prospect of a reasonable audience size at a reasonable cost, for the limited budget.

Direct mail

This is a tremendous force, growing fast, and one with a wide range of practical values:

■ the ability to go direct to the target
■ high selectivity of audience
■ the growing ability to select ever more precisely
■ the ability to match message to audience
■ flexibility, by time, audience, message, area
■ the ability to raise a response.

A key value of direct mail is that it is *testable*. Much direct mail is tested on a small sample, often comparatively, before being extended.

Direct mail lends itself to follow-up activity, lead generation, sales enquiry or enquiry for further information.

It has become increasingly sophisticated, especially since the growth of database marketing and the development of database systems.

An effective database is at the heart of direct marketing, and database availability is becoming easier and more practical than ever.

In many areas (such as direct marketing or charities) direct mail may not only communicate but sell.

It is valuable (if expensive) for many consumer categories, but is of outstanding importance in business-to-business activities, where it is often the prime communications tool.

Directories

There are over 5000 directories or yearbooks, and they offer a category in their own right. Directories have the following advantages:

- they are retained for long periods
- they are a prime source among readers for information and reference
- there is high coverage, and high frequency of message
- they are highly selective, providing specialist coverage against specialist industries and audiences.

There are two groups:

1. consumer directories (of which the two largest are telephone directories and *Yellow Pages*), including local authority publications
2. business-to-business or trade directories.

For targeted audiences with targeted messages, directories can be highly cost-effective and provide substantial pulling power. As one example, the *Floodlight* directory (covering education courses in London) leads to literally thousands of contacts by students with colleges.

Outdoor and transportation

This is a medium-sized category restricted by the quantity of sites available under public planning regulations. This category falls into two sectors:

1. outdoor:
   - commercial poster sites
   - Ad Shel bus stop sites
2. transportation:
   - sites on trains
   - sites in railway stations
   - sites in the interior of buses
   - sites on the exterior of buses
   - sites in tube stations
   - sites in tube trains.

The sites vary by size, and a large range of sizes may be offered. The suppliers of these spaces will be contractors, acting in the case of transport on behalf of transport authorities, although some transport bodies still sell space direct.

While it is considered that outdoor does not have the immediacy and impact of, say, TV, it nevertheless offers its own substantial values:

- wide geographical coverage
- the ability to localise or concentrate in areas
- very high repetition: passers-by return to the site frequently; this is especially true of transportation advertising
- ability to locate near types of distributor
- relative economy
- high-aggregate audiences.

Outdoor can be a strong selective medium for certain types of markets; for example petroleum, automotive, alcohol, fashion, entertainment.

Radio

This has grown substantially as a commercial medium, due to a rapid extension of commercial as against BBC stations. Radio, too, splits into two sectors:

1. local
2. national.

At one time, British commercial radio was entirely local, but a variety of national stations has now come into being.

Radio, by definition, cannot show products or demonstrate, but sound can be used to a highly creative degree. Among benefits are:

- the ability to localise or regionalise
- the ability to accumulate a national audience
- reasonable aggregate cover, albeit limited per individual transmission
- flexibility and speed.

The medium is beneficial for local advertisers, for short-term news and announcement, for dealer and distributor support, for area activities and for test-market purpose.

Cinema

After an enormous decline following the advent of TV, the cinema has rallied in the immediate past and presents a reasonable audience level in cities and larger towns. Many smaller towns and country areas still do not possess a cinema.

■ Cinema gives sound coverage of younger (16–24) age groups.
■ Cinema has impact, and a captive audience.
■ It has colour, sound, movement and the ability to demonstrate.
■ It can be localised, if required.

Because of its audience profile, cinema is frequently used by local advertisers, entertainment or catering outlets, and by fashion, alcohol, toiletries and cosmetic products aimed at younger audiences.

Exhibitions

A major medium, again operating in two categories:

1. consumer
2. trade and business to business.

They may be mounted in two ways:

1. using exhibition space provided by commercial contractors
2. in-house operation.

Commercial exhibitions will use the range of exhibition venues now available across the country. Well-known examples are Olympia, Earls Court and Wembley in London and the National Exhibition Centre in Birmingham. The exhibition organisers mount the exhibition, attract the visitors and provide space for exhibitors.

Most exhibitions are organised around a specific subject area or theme. Self-operated exhibitions may include:

■ the use of mobile units eg caravans or converted buses
■ 'roadshows' moving from town to town
■ use of local hotel space, or other public buildings.

The exhibitor is solus, but has the additional overhead of mounting the show.

Values of exhibitions are considerable, as long as costs do not go out of control. Exhibitions provide:

▧ specific audiences for specific markets (The Boat Show, Interbuild, The Direct Marketing Show etc)
▧ the opportunity to make personal contact
▧ the potential to take orders and sell.

Indeed, exhibition stands may be self-financing if sufficient orders can be obtained at the exhibition.

Telemarketing

The use of the telephone for commercial purposes has spread very rapidly, and is forecast to grow still further as part of the coming telecommunications expansion. There are two types of telemarketing:

1. inbound: where respondents telephone the advertiser
2. outbound: where the advertiser telephones out to the customer.

A wide and flexible range of facilities is provided by the telephone companies, with inbound services ranging from free calls, to national calls at a local price, to calls where the advertiser may obtain an income.

Telemarketing is particularly potent in business-to-business markets, where there is a defined target group which may be difficult to reach in any other way.

Telemarketing offers a clear number of benefits:

▧ the ability to target selectively, using a variety of lists
▧ personal contact
▧ the ability to operate nationally, or to localise
▧ the telephone may be used to sell, or to develop sales leads, or to make appointments for the sales force, or to follow up on previous contacts
▧ it is highly visible and can be mounted rapidly.

There is a considerable wastage factor but telemarketing needs to be evaluated in overall terms, as a total ratio of conversions to calls, rather than looking at the success rate of separate calls one by one.

Electronic

While the TV has emerged as an all-purpose communications centre for the home, the PC may well be the key communication tool of the future, capable of multifunctions, rather more than the TV set. A key and decisive feature is that it is *interactive*. The PC thus offers a whole new dimension, with boundless possibilities.

The PC becomes not just a tool for data processing but for communication. Associated with the PC is the growth of the World Wide Web and the Internet. While limited in terms of penetration, a clear range of benefits is offered in the future:

▩ messages can cross frontiers
▩ interaction and self-selection of products and services
▩ flexibility and speed
▩ targeting
▩ low cost.

THE FACTORS TO CONSIDER

The advertiser or the agency has defined a media brief, and has listed the range of media available. But, what should those media provide? What is it that the advertiser should look for?

Different circumstances require different benefits, but in overall terms there are certain basic criteria the advertiser needs to consider when seeking to put together a media plan. These are the media essentials.

Coverage
How much of the target audience does the medium cover? The advertiser should not just be looking for sheer size, or circulation, but coverage. The aim is to cover as much of the target audience as fully, as economically and as comfortably as possible.

Readership or viewership
To assess coverage, the advertiser needs not only to know the circulation of a magazine or the number of sets switched on to a TV programme, but the full *audience* of those media; in a magazine not just the copies sold but the number of readers, or the size of the readership; for TV, the size of viewership. And so on for the other media.

Frequency
How often is the message seen? What is the frequency of messages delivered? In cases where repetition is required, frequency is a key factor. But there is a balance to be struck. The advertiser has to make a decision: is it better to deliver several messages to a smaller audience (by running a number of insertions in one publication) or to deliver fewer messages to a wider audience? On a limited, given budget this judgement may to a large extent depend on what is called for in the media objectives.

Opportunity to see
The gross number of media or of space insertions is not the key requirement. The advertiser needs to establish if possible a high rate of 'opportunities to see' – OTSs. This factors out the number of insertions against the size of the audience and establishes the average number of times an average member of the target audience has the opportunity to see a message. This is the best measurement of the achievement of an advertising schedule.

Value and cost
On a set budget, the advertiser will presumably look for value for money and cost benefits by selecting those media which deliver the best audience size with the greatest cost value.

Economy
Different media cost different sums. It is important to evaluate their comparative economy, one against the other. The method here is to factor out their *cost per '000*. This takes a unit of space (say, one-column centimetre) and divides the cost of this unit into the number of thousands of readers. If a unit of space costs £10 and there are 10,000 readers then the cost per '000 is £1. Using the cost per '000 measurement, it is possible to compare media. Other things being equal (which they are not always) a low cost per '000 is the desired objective.

Timing and duration
These may be major issues. If buying days, for example Saturdays, are key, then the advertiser must use those media which can provide concentration on a day-by-day basis. Again, campaigns may need to be of a certain duration for which some media are more suitable than others.

Response factors

Response mechanisms such as a coupon or a telephone number may be necessary. Again, certain media behave better for response messages.

Impact

OTS is an 'opportunity to see'. But the advertiser may demand *real* seeing. Not just an opportunity. So does the medium have *impact*? Or the potential for actual seeing or viewing? Media may provide such opportunities in particular ways:

▓ *Size:* a large size may be more visible than a smaller. But, is it better to have fewer large sizes or more smaller sizes? Whatever the choice, in all cases the advertiser must stipulate a size.
▓ *Position:* better positions may have better visibility: poster sites near a shopping centre, a solus front page space in a newspaper, a TV spot in the main evening TV news broadcast, inside the front cover of a magazine. But again, if a premium is to be paid for special positions, is it worth it?
▓ *Colour:* impact can be gained from colour. How much is it worth?
▓ *Timing:* this factor again can achieve impact. Advertising at the right moment may ensure greater attention from the audience.

Editorial environment

Theoretically, an advertisement gains from the surrounding editorial. It gains credibility, or enhanced status or greater awareness. So, a fashion product will benefit from *Vogue* magazine, garden seeds from using the gardening press – so long as those media do not carry too much advertising, or are not too crowded and cluttered. The challenge for example is to use *The Architects' Journal* for its prestige and its targeting but to handle the fact that at the peak season it could carry a hundred or more advertisements.

Flexibility

What are the cancellation timings for the media? How quickly can space be bought? How quickly can advertising appear? How quickly can it be abandoned?

Trade and sales force influence

Where distributors or sales force staff are important factors, their attitude to media should be remembered – by the choice of media which appeal to them and which they will support.

INFORMATION TO USE

In order to make the final selection, the advertiser may call for detailed data or information to assist in the decision. Indeed, the advertiser must demand certain basic facts, because otherwise the judgement will be extremely difficult. One of the current features of the media scene is the wide availability of media statistics, and the availability of sources for those statistics. Essential elements to know include:

■ *Circulation:* the measurement of circulation sizes, the number of copies sold.
■ *Readers:* overall readers, and readers per copy.
■ *Viewerships and listenerships:* the number of viewers or listeners for a TV or radio programme or commercial.
■ *Audience composition:* what is the profile of the medium's clients? By occupation, income, seniority or age, sex, demographic grouping.
■ *Area profile:* what is the geographical split of the publication, or TV station? Where are its area strengths and weaknesses?
■ *Cost:* the capital cost of space.
■ *Cost per '000:* cost per '000 readers or viewers.
■ *Trends:* what is the readership or viewership trend of that particular medium? Is it increasing or decreasing in size? What are the forecasts?

Sources for such data include auditing services such as the Audit Bureau of Circulation. Large-scale industry-wide research surveys are available which estimate press readership, TV viewership or poster audiences. Or there are surveys and analyses carried out by the individual media themselves. Media associations or advertising agencies have access and can advise, while the individual media will provide media packs giving basic statistics and background information about themselves.

HOW TO SELECT

So far we have established that:

■ the advertiser sets out a brief

■ a large number of media options may exist
■ the advertiser may look for a variety of media values
■ there is a variety of information to help.

The main step now is actually to select the most suitable media: the moment of decision. To do this, there are two steps to be taken.

1. defining candidate media
2. eliminating the least likely, and so refining down to the most likely.

That is, media selection is generally a process of elimination.

Candidate media

Which media exist which can properly achieve the media target? That is, which can provide:

■ a suitable audience profile
■ suitable coverage
■ with suitable frequency
■ plus suitable visibility
■ at an economic price
■ with the right timing
■ with a helpful media environment
■ and which are able to convey the right creative message.

To answer this, there may be just one, simple, obvious, immediate candidate. Or there may be just a few. Or there may be a whole host.

Advertiser Jones wishes to recruit for factory staff. The local newspaper is well read. It is the obvious choice.

Advertiser Smith wishes to advertise a specialist software package to solicitors on a limited budget and in a professional way. Various means are apparent: the use of legal magazines such as the Law Society's *Gazette*; direct mail; possibly telemarketing; trade directories. The range is not limitless. One or other or a mix may be selected.

Advertiser Brown runs a local restaurant. Although the budget is small, there is apparently a huge number of possibilities: the local newspaper; the local cinema; posters; sites at the local railway station; *Yellow Pages*; local radio, if it is small scale enough; direct mail to business customers; leafleting. Here, advertiser Brown has an abundance of choice and will have severely to limit the selection.

The media plan will list the possibilities, then abandon some.

Process of elimination

Sifting and evaluating may be done by computer or it may be done by human brain and judgement. In essence, the different media categories need to be compared, and then the specific media within them. The advertiser or agency will define and compare:

- audience, and target selectivity
- size of audience delivered, and audience coverage
- cost per '000 messages
- comparative capital costs
- possible visibility and impact of the message
- the mix which best optimises *reach* and *frequency*
- any timing advantages or limitation.

One by one the weaker performing media will be rejected until a final single candidate or shortlisted mix of media remain. This shortlist will not only show the suggested media, but the best size and most practical size of space to use.

Here the plan must carry out the final balancing trick by identifying a media combination, which balances out the three major factors:

1. size of audience
2. frequency of message
3. size and position of message.

So, the final media plan establishes a pattern of which media to use, how large the space will be, and the number of advertisements to appear. The media plan is a combination of elements, totalling the budget set.

Space size

All media come in a very large range of space sizes, from very small to very large. Apart from deciding which media to select, the advertiser must also decide which size to use.

The media will usually indicate on their rate card which sizes are available.

Newspapers usually split their space sizes by columns and centimetres, from one single column centimetre upwards. So typical sizes might be:

- 2 cm × 1 column
- 5 cm × 2 columns
- 24 cm × 4 columns

Magazines split their space by proportions of page. For example:

- ⅛ page
- ¼ page
- ½ page
- whole page

Posters operate 'sheet size', multiple of a single sheet. For example:

- 48 sheet (20′ × 10′)
- 32 sheet (13′4″ × 10′)
- 16 sheet (6′8″ × 10′)
- 4 sheet (40″ × 60″)

Radio, cinema and television operate by multiples of seconds. Television normally offers, 10, 20, 30 and 60 second time-lengths.

The selection of a particular size of space depends on four things. These are:

1. The length of the message. How much time or space will it need?
2. The desire for impact. A reasonable space size will be needed to be physically seen.
3. The budget. How large a size can be afforded?
4. The balance between size and the other elements of coverage and frequency.

The advertiser will have to arrive at the most comfortable compromise.

There is a tendency to spread advertising across a range of media, to provide wider coverage. Various insertions in each medium can provide a high message frequency, so raising the message's prominence. But usually a compromise has to take place, as the advertiser generally cannot afford everything, so must calculate a reasonable *balance*. A sound, workable number of media, reasonable frequency and space size, not the maximum, is the most sensible outcome for the budget.

The final plan

From all this work, a final media plan will be drawn up. It will indicate the media selected and how they work.

- ■ *Media:* which media will be used.
- ■ *Space size:* the size of the space in each.
- ■ *Frequency:* the number of appearances in each.
- ■ *Timing:* when each advertisement is to appear.
- ■ *Cost:* how much each insertion costs, and how much is the total.

Only now is it time to go away and buy the space.

MEDIA PLANNING CHECKLIST

■ Who is the target? Where are they?
■ How often should they be reached?
■ When should they be reached?
■ How extensive is the message?
■ What environment is required?
■ What response is required?
■ What are the budgetary limitations?
■ What media are appropriate?

	Size of audience	Profile of audience	Size and cost of space	Cost per '000
Media type or category				
Medium within the category				

■ What information is available?
■ What further information is needed?
■ What are the comparative costs and benefits in these media of:
  – colour?
  – special positions?
  – special timings?

5

How to Buy Media Space

WHO DOES THE BUYING?

Having planned the media space, it is necessary to buy it. Planning is an internal exercise; buying means going out into the market-place and dealing with the media. Planning deals with the theory, buying encounters the actuality. The advertiser must first decide *who* will actually purchase the space that is required. There are three different ways of doing this:

1. buying the advertisement space directly
2. using an advertising agency
3. using a media independent.

It is rare to have a mix of all three.

Advertiser buying direct

The general principle of advertising placement is that the media will give a recognised advertising agency a commission to cover its costs, but will not do so for an advertiser direct. Therefore an advertiser will not benefit financially from booking direct, so might as well use an agency The agency service 'comes free'.

There are, however, a variety of circumstances when the adver-tiser may find it helpful to book direct, and some do so. It might be cheaper to buy space than use an agency, especially a London-based agency.

Discount arrangements

Various media *do* allow advertisers a discount direct. The theoretical commission system may not specify this, but it is possible in practice. Advertisers in highly technical markets, for example, where there is one leading magazine, may forge a strong relationship with that magazine and be able to agree some sort of rebate scheme.

Size of spend

Advertisers who are large users of certain media may gain leverage and use their position to extract commissions, by sheer weight.

Complex products

In highly complex or highly technical fields, an advertiser may find it easier and more reliable to deal with the media direct and then produce the advertisement direct.

Small advertisers

Private individuals or very small advertisers may find it less bothersome just to deal with the media direct. They might not, anyway, find an advertising agency willing to handle them.

But the downside of all this is the time and overheads involved, and the possible lack of expertise of the advertiser. For this reason, large-scale campaigns usually rely on some kind of outside specialist for purchasing their space.

Use of an advertising agency

Many advertisers use advertising agencies to purchase media for them. The agency provides expertise. Its services may come free and (a growing benefit) the agency may offer the advertiser better credit terms than may be obtained from the media themselves.

The media may want payment up front, or in 14 days, or at best in 30 days from the date of the advertisement. The agencies, on the other hand, often invoice clients in one consolidated invoice at the end of each month and allow 30 days' credit after that.

Use of media independent

These organisations buy and sell media only. They may place the advertiser's space, take a percentage of the commission and then rebate the balance back to the advertiser. Thus it is a cheaper arrangement.

The media independent is a specialist, with considerable expertise, often using their weight of media purchasing to gain extra highly favourable space costs.

On the other hand, smaller advertisers may be too small for them, advertisers with complex schedules or using small spaces may be too complex and fragmented for them, and advertisers with a high workload may be too expensive for them. Again, media independents may demand tougher credit terms than full-service agencies. And the advertiser will have to find someone else to do the creative work product by product.

An area where media independents have made substantial inroads is that of the larger company, splitting its business among a range of advertising agencies. Here the media independent can provide central buying across the company with the agencies producing the creative work product by product.

The final decision is one of judgement. A rule of thumb might be:

■ private individuals – buy direct
■ very small advertisers – buy direct
■ highly specialist advertisers – buy direct
■ medium-sized and mainstream advertisers – use an advertising agency
■ cases where creative work is primary – use an advertising agency
■ larger companies – compare an agency with a media independent
■ multi-brand companies – use a media independent for central buying.

DECIDING ON A SCHEDULE

The media plan needs to be turned into an advertising schedule. Buying is done off a schedule. Once the media plan has been agreed, the advertising agency (we will assume for the sake of simplicity in the rest of this chapter that an agency is being used) will produce a schedule for the client. This should come in two stages:

1. draft schedule, for approval
2. bought schedule, as purchased from the media.

			PRESS SCHEDULE			
COMPANY					DATE	
PRODUCT						

PUBLICATION	CIRCULATION	SPACE SIZE AND POSITION	COST PER INSERTION	NUMBER OF INSERTIONS	GROSS COST	DATES TO APPEAR
				TOTAL VAT	COST EXTRA	

Figure 5.1 *Advertisement schedule*

In practice, these are usually identical – but are not always so. A schedule will cover all the details of the space to be bought. Where the advertiser buys space direct, it would still be helpful to draw up a similar schedule. A basic schedule format would be as in the illustration. See Figure 5.1.

Details would be typed in, including suggested dates of appearance. VAT would be shown as a total. A column could be added if required indicating standard advertising agency commissions.

The schedule forms a contract between client and agency. Similar schedule formats are used for outdoor advertising, TV etc, and are often printed out on computerised scheduling systems, rather than manually.

NEGOTIATING SPACE

Space now needs to be bought, and it is usually bought from the advertisement department of a medium and from an individual media representative in that department. The media buyer will look for:

- space available at the time required or
- space available at the next best time
- a good position
- an option which may be held open for an initial period, if further consideration is needed
- economy possibilities.

PRICE NEGOTIATION

Media will operate standard rate cards, with basic advertisement rates which will run over a period – often 12 months. These rates will cover a permutation of charges across advertisement space:

- basic rates, on a run of paper basis
- rates for different standard sizes
- extra premiums for special positions or fixing times
- rates for colour advertising
- discounts for buying space in bulk, eg for a fixed number of insertions or a fixed volume of space.

The agency will try to buy at best possible terms. It will try to take advantage of any discount potential and will look for other benefits. For example:

- special positions at run of paper rates
- special days at run of week rates
- volume or frequency discounts when the actual purchase falls a little short of the minimum discount level.

Certain special prices may operate additionally. For example:

- test market rates, for new products
- charity rates, for recognised charities
- local advertiser rates, for purely local advertisers.

There will be different rate cards for different aspects of the publication. For example:

- display advertising sections
- classified advertising sections
- specialist sections, such as education courses or recruitment.

As well as the volume discounts on offer through the rate card, the media buyer will also look for other price concessions. Some media may be persuaded to offer further price cuts to ensure the media booking, or to attract advertisers to last-minute space which otherwise would go unsold.

The recent past has seen a high volume of media dealing. Many advertisers have bought at very low rates. But advertisers must not automatically expect price reductions. The basic tool is still the rate card as published. Deals are harder to get than often imagined. Remember:

■ smaller advertisers are less well placed and may not have the influence
■ highly popular or successful media will deal less
■ many media do not deal at all
■ where demand exceeds supply, rates may go up rather than down
■ some conditions for granting rebates may be more than an advertiser can achieve: a continuous campaign at high frequency is one thing, a single booking quite another
■ those media which discount the most are often the least desirable.

Good positions and assured dates of appearance are often better than a nominal rate reduction. What counts most is *value* rather than low cost!

THE PURCHASE

When agreed, the agency issues the media with a space order. There are separate space orders for all the media on the schedule. If buying direct, the advertiser too should issue a space order. They provide a formal, detailed confirmation of what is to be bought. This can be seen in Figure 5.2.

The agency will invoice the client in the terms of this order, and will check the media invoices to see if they correspond with the order. Similar formats will be used for radio, TV and so on. The medium will issue an acknowledgement of this order.

The advertiser must bear in mind the problem of cancellation dates. Within a certain space of time from the appearance of the advertising, the space will be non-cancellable. Once cancellation

```
┌──────────────────────────────────────────────────────────────┐
│                        SPACE ORDER                             │
│                                          Order No _____    │
│                                                                │
│  Publication _____      Advertiser _____     │
│                                                                │
│  Address _____        Product _____      │
│                                                                │
│                                  Date _____       │
│                                                                │
│  Space/position _____                       │
│                                                                │
│  Rate per insertion _____                       │
│                                                                │
│  Number of insertions _____                        │
│                                                                │
│  Dates of insertion _____                        │
│                                                                │
│  Rate of agency commission_____                          │
│                                                                │
│                          Please provide two voucher copies     │
└──────────────────────────────────────────────────────────────┘
```

Figure 5.2   *Space order*

date has passed, the advertiser must pay for the space and is committed to it. It becomes a binding contract.

Cancellation dates vary from medium to medium. For some press media cancellation can be made within days of the issue date. For other media (eg some colour space in magazines) space may not be cancelled within six months of the issue date.

If the product or the budget are doubtful, advertisers should not use media with long cancellation dates.

Once booked, however, media space may be altered – so long as the cancellation dates are observed. Details may be varied, and to achieve this, formal amendment orders should be issued, as seen in Figure 5.3. Full details of the required change would be shown. Once again, invoices would be checked against any agreed amendments.

REFINING THE SCHEDULE

While many schedules appear as originally planned, it may be possible to evaluate results and to refine the media bookings in the light of experience. For example, space sizes may be varied, especially for newspapers. Or positions may be moved, from a run of paper to a fixed space. Or days of appearance may alter.

MEDIA AMENDMENT

Amendment No _____

Publication _____   Advertiser _____

Address _____   Product _____

Date _____

Our Space Order No _____

Please amend as follows:

Figure 5.3 *Amendment order*

Similarly, within TV, policy may alter from buying off-peak to buying peak, or from buying across the week to buying nearer to weekends. Time lengths would probably stay constant.

The aim is to achieve a balance. Too frequent a change would dislocate the schedule and fragment its effect. But never seeking an improvement would fail to utilise experience or learn from results.

This general process applies across the range of media-buying situations, from display advertising to classified or semi-classified, from recruitment sections to holidays, and travel to education. The process is:

■ selection of space
■ negotiating the space
■ negotiating terms
■ issuing a space order
■ issuing an amendment
■ refining as a schedule proceeds.

Many advertisements, such as for recruitment, are one-off and the process of refinement by definition cannot apply. But here, too, previous experience may be brought to bear on buying new space in the future.

MONITORING

The advertiser will require proof of actual appearance. Obviously, this is necessary to justify payment. Proof is easier to obtain with print media. Here copies of actual newspapers or magazines can be obtained (although not always easily available) and checked.

Many clients will require print voucher copies to accompany the agency invoices. The vouchers will be checked, to compare details of space obtained as against the space orders and the schedule.

There is greater difficulty with TV, but the TV research system can produce a printout of spots appearing which will act as a certificate of transmission or confirmation of TV appearance. The same applies to radio.

A sub-sample of poster sites can be monitored, again by a standard research service, to assess appearance of posters.

EVALUATION

Actual results should be measured to evaluate the media achievement of a schedule. While this may not be possible or necessary in all cases (for one-off advertisements or special schedules) it can be helpful and informative with ongoing campaigns or high levels of expenditure.

Such campaigns should be examined in two ways:

1. in terms of numbers achieved
2. in terms of quality obtained.

If possible, the size of the potential audience should be calculated in advance, in terms of:

▓ total size
▓ percentage cover of the target audience
▓ average frequency or number of messages delivered
▓ cost per '000 audience.

Once the campaign has run, these numbers should be looked at again, at least in terms of what has been delivered.

In some media categories, the situation is short term.

Unless the media mix changes during the course of the campaign it is likely that press achievement will be as per the original estimate, failing cancellations or missed insertions.

For posters, the number of posters appearing needs to be checked against the preliminary estimate.

For TV and radio, total audience size may be measured against the actual spots transmitted and the actual audience obtained.

Media research data for each media category will be used. Any deviation from the forecast can be spotted and in particular actual cost per '000 audience data can be calculated for TV and radio off the details of the actual spots.

'Quality' is a somewhat more hazardous concept. But it may be possible to evolve a system of grading, given a definition of what quality can represent.

For press advertising, for example, the ideal might be to obtain positions on the front half of the newspaper, or the right-hand side, or at the top of the page. Calculations can be made of achievement against this theoretical standard of press advertisement space quality. In other words, a stipulation of quality space or time is agreed, and an analysis made of the ratios of achievement.

In some markets (eg direct marketing or mail order) it may be possible to gain more specific data, such as:

■ number of enquiries
■ cost per enquiry
■ number of applications for goods
■ cost per application
■ value of sales, per applicant
■ ratio of value: advertising spend
■ follow-on sales per applicant.

From this can be factored out those media which performed best against any particular chosen criteria.

All this depends on the provision of data, which is not always available, or economic to assemble, or usable. But where practicable, evaluation of performance is a helpful exercise – at least for next time round.

INVOICING

Where an advertiser does not have a credit arrangement, they may be asked to pay in advance. Where there is a credit arrangement, they will be asked to pay promptly by the end of 30 days. Or 15 days in the case of TV. Where billed via an agency or media independent, payment again is called for within 30 days.

However, where there is an error on the invoice or where the agency believes the medium has made a mistake or has failed to deliver properly, compensation may be sought. Invoice errors may be settled by a credit note, and inadequate space or reproduction failure may be settled by a reduction in price.

Free space is more difficult to obtain. The media concede price reductions slowly and with natural reluctance.

MEDIA RELATIONS

One of the strengths of advertising agencies or media independents is their knowledge of the media and their knowledge of media people. Good media relations are essential in obtaining satisfactory offers and satisfactory service.

The agency needs to keep close to the media, to know what is going on, and to know how best to speak to media staff. It should certainly know the characteristics of the main media, and be able to communicate with them both at an operational and senior management level. But the agency must not be so close as to lose its objectivity.

A question often asked is, how far the advertiser should be involved with the media direct, even if using an agency. Commonsense should prevail on this point. When using an agency there is a danger of confusion or duplication of effort. This must be avoided. The agency should lead on buying. But if the advertiser operates in a specialist area, or uses a limited number of major publications, it may be helpful (and indeed inevitable) for the advertiser to get to know the key media too – just so long as both the advertiser and the agency communicate with each other about their contacts.

MEDIA BUYING CHECKLIST

■ Which are the media you will use?
■ Size, by circulation, readership, audience, viewership.
■ Audience composition, by category of audience.
■ Coverage of the target audience.
■ Size to be bought.
■ Comparative costs and values of alternative sizes.
■ Positions.
■ Timing, by month, week, day – or hour.
■ Rate card cost of space.
■ Actual cost of space.
■ Saving achieved.
■ Discounts obtained, other discounts available.
■ Number of insertions or appearances.
■ Cost per '000 messages.
■ Average frequency or opportunity to see.
■ Colour versus monochrome/colour facilities.
■ Payment terms and credit facility.
■ Voucher and monitoring system.
■ Optimum space, position or time required.
■ Actual delivered.
■ Cancellation dates and copy dates.

6

Developing the Advertising Message

IT IS THE MESSAGE THAT COUNTS

Advertising sets out to inform and persuade. The content of advertising communications is at the core of what advertising does. This aspect is often called 'creative', as in the creative department of an advertising agency, and the message or advertisement content is called 'the creative work'. Some advertisements are more creative than others, and the phrase may seem somewhat pretentious. But it is obvious that the advertising message must attract the audience, engage their attention, sharpen their interest and give them a strong feeling about the product or service. To do this requires insight, imagination and, indeed, a good measure of creative skill.

Advertisements are an exercise in writing and design, in words and pictures, and require considerable verbal and pictorial abilities. The difference between one campaign and another is often in the quality of this creative input. An advertisement is only as good as the strength and effectiveness of its message. This is what communication is about.

THE PROCESS

Although literary and artistic skills are required, developing creative communication is a commercial process, requiring professionalism and expertise, and progress in controlled stages. The main ingredients are as follows:

Agreeing a brief

Just as a formal media brief is necessary in order to develop a media schedule, so a creative brief is helpful to set out the requisites for a communications message. This will state the main elements needed and will act as the reference point for the subsequent creative work.

Formulating a creative strategy

In the light of the brief agreed at the outset, a strategy follows, which will establish the general direction of the campaign, the overall proposition, or product attribute to be featured, the kind of promise or appeal to be made.

Developing a concept

The essence of an advertisement is the idea behind it, what it has to say to the audience. The main, overlying idea, the theme of the message, the advertising *concept* is the central point of an advertising campaign. Advertising campaigns stand or fall, work or fail, by the strength or weakness of their basic concept.

The execution

Once a concept has been evolved, it must then be worked out in a fuller form – a finished advertisement. It is put into words or pictures – slogans, text, body-copy, illustrations.

Producing a final advertisement

Having been agreed by the advertiser, words and pictures have to be turned into a form where they can be printed or transmitted. They are made into artwork or film. This itself progresses through two stages:

1. *Artwork:* shooting photographs, drawing illustrations, drawing up borders or logotypes and so on and typesetting the text.
2. *Advertisement production:* producing the physical material that will be sent to the media for them to publish or transmit. For

press this will mean typesetting and film-making (where news-papers print from film); for posters this will mean printing the posters; for TV it means shooting the TV commercial and providing prints or copy videos for the TV stations; for radio it will mean recording sessions and the production of copy tapes.

From the point of view of the communications manager, this process will go through a series of decision stages. Approval needs to be given at each point and the communications manager must remain in control throughout. The stages are:

1. Developing the creative brief.
2. Agreeing the creative strategy.
3. Approving the creative concept. This may be done separately, or as part of the next stage (4).
4. Examining and approving the finished advertisement. This is done in different forms for different media categories, as follows:
   - press, posters, direct mail: layouts for the design and draft copy for the text
   - TV and cinema: a rough soundtrack, a script, a storyboard (or drawn approximation of the visual) and sometimes a rough-shot pilot track.
5. Agreeing the produced version. This has two stages:
   - press, posters, direct mail, directories: first, agreeing any photography or illustrations or other kinds of finished artwork; then, developing and approving a proof of the type-setting and final printed form
   - TV, cinema and radio: first developing and agreeing produc-tion elements such as casting, costumes, set design, locations and also producing and agreeing any music that has to be recorded; then shooting the final film or recording the final soundtrack and again agreeing it before transmission.

Each stage needs to have a formal and precise timetable, so that the complete enterprise progresses smoothly on course.

WHO DOES WHAT?

Advertisers may develop communications messages in a variety of ways. But there are four basic ways usually adopted.

In-house

The advertiser may quite simply do it all himself. Where a message is brief or resources are limited, the advertiser may just quickly think of the words, produce an illustration, and get these set up by the newspaper providing the media space. This saves bother, argument and time. A local retailer may decide on a sales advertisement, draft out the wording, find a photograph of the product, jot down an indication of what the advertisement should look like and then send them round to the local newspaper, which will offer a production facility. There is nothing wrong in this, and many smaller advertisers do it.

Alternatively, the advertiser may be large enough to operate an in-house creative facility – a design studio, for example. Certain kinds of advertiser (larger retailers, motorcar companies, engineering or chemical companies, for example) find it expedient to operate a studio in order to design display material, or catalogues or price lists, or house magazines. They can also be used to develop advertisements.

The growth of desk-top publishing systems and the availability at low cost of suitable computers (eg the Apple Mac) and graphics packages make it easier to produce in-house artwork to a reasonable standard.

While useful as a fast and economic resource, in-house facilities may nevertheless be limited in terms of fresh ideas, or creative originality.

The advertising agency

Traditionally, the bulk of larger-scale campaigns has been done through advertising agencies, for the sake of specialist skills, provision of talent, and general creative know-how.

Creative groups or consultancies

An increasing number of advertisers (though by no means the majority) combine the use of a media independent to buy space with a creative consultancy to develop the message. A large number of specialist consultancies or creative groups now exist, especially in London. They will do the complete advertisement development job, for a fee.

Finished art studios also offer creative origination. Where an advertiser uses a design studio to produce brochures or catalogues, it may be convenient to combine this with the production of advertisements too.

Specialist creative work

Advertisers may use several methods simultaneously. It is common for an advertiser to use an advertising agency plus a specialist creative source for particular kinds of specialised activity. For example:

■ *advertising agency:* advertisements for the main media, press, TV, radio etc
■ *exhibition designer:* specialist design for exhibition stands
■ *direct mail writer:* a specialist in writing mailshots.

The advertiser will select whichever methods or combination of methods is easiest, quickest, and cheapest. Above all, the method which produces the most satisfactory results. Here it is fair to observe that most advertisers find the advertising agency still to be the most convenient resource.

BRIEFING THE CREATIVE WORK

The process begins with the brief. Of course, many advertisements are one-off, or casual or even accidental. But they all should begin with a formal instruction to someone to develop the necessary creative proposal. The instruction may be verbal and short, or it may be substantial and fully deliberated. For major campaigns, and for large expenditures of money, a clear and decisive brief is absolutely essential. This is the responsibility of the advertiser. Advertising agencies or specialist creative groups may respond to a brief, comment on it and perhaps suggest amendments to it, but it is bad practice to allow them to dictate the brief. This has ultimately to be the prerogative of the advertiser. In the end, it is the advertiser who must have the control.

The brief lays down the essence of what the message must achieve, as shown in Figure 6.1. It needs to be produced by the communications manager, but also checked and agreed with the corporate management and other sections of the organisation in order to avoid disagreements later on.

CREATIVE BRIEF

Product_____

Period of advertising

Objectives of the campaign

Target audience

What the audience now knows about the product

What the audience now feels about the product

What we want the audience to know about the product

What we want the audience to feel about the product

The main features of the product

Main customer requirements

Main features of competitor   (a)

                                     (b)

Positioning of the product required

Date when the campaign begins   ends

Figure 6.1   *The creative brief*

THE GENERAL STRATEGY

The brief states what is wanted. The question above all is: what to communicate? The creative strategy points to the main features of communication, *what* the message is to convey and which elements or attributes of the product should be used or emphasised to convey this.

Product 1
Advertising objective: to achieve a reputation as the highest quality plain chocolate assortment.

Proposed strategy:to show the high social acceptability of the product and its immediate appeal as a gift.

Product 2

Advertising objective: to become known as the provider of a wide range of distance learning courses, answering any educational need.

Proposed strategy: to major on the number of courses offered, to group them, and to show how each group completely covers that particular field.

Product 3

Advertising objective: to obtain a high rate of enquiries for the main holiday brochure and a high awareness as a provider of attractive mass-market Mediterranean holidays.

Proposed strategy: to emphasise price, by showing price/value to key destinations, with a supporting statement of the number of destinations covered and listing the UK airports from which the holidays can be taken.

Product 4

Advertising objective: to help achieve strong traffic through the store and maintain identity as the leading retailer of top quality bedding.

Proposed strategy: emphasis on the top-end of the range of products and superior stockholding of styles, sizes and firmnesses.

The strategy needs to identify the specific direction the message should take:

■ What element about the product or service will isolate it from the competition and make it seem special?
■ What attribute will most answer the customer's motivation?
■ What aspect of the product or service will gain greatest attention?
■ Where does its prime benefit lie?
■ What is it about the product or the service that will sell it most surely?

The strategy will draw this out, and concentrate upon it.

Only when the strategy is clear, unmistakable and generally agreed will the advertising process move forward.

THE CENTRAL CONCEPT

Advertisements have to work fast, they have to work quickly and they have to work simply. There may be two situations in which an advertising campaign is placed, in relation to the audience.

Firstly, there is the situation where the audience is looking for this kind of message, wants to find it, will think it helpful and may act upon it. They may well search it out.

This is the situation for many kinds of advertising. When interest rates change, people may want to see what rates banks are now offering. When the holiday season comes round, people being to look for information on possible holiday venues. When your drain is blocked, you may look up *Yellow Pages* to see who is the nearest drain service. When you need a prescription filled, you may look at a directory for details of a late night pharmacy. When your car begins to fail, you will look around for details of a possible replacement and for the locations of suitable dealers.

In which cases, advertising can be direct, basic, informative and flag down the audience already in the mood to take an interest.

Unfortunately, this is not the position for most products most of the time. People do not generally read newspapers for the advertisements or watch TV for the commercials. Many direct mailshots are thrown into the dustbin. Posters are unheeded as people walk by.

Audiences do not seek out most kinds of advertisement and indeed often try to avoid them. In which case the advertiser has a considerable job to do. The priority is to appeal, to stand out, to have something relevant to say.

The advertising strategy is merely a statement of an intention. It now has to be turned into a live piece of communication, one which will gain attention, be looked at, convey a point and be remembered. That is the job of the advertising concept.

The concept represents the centre of the message. It is the idea behind the message. It is the proposition that is being made. When the advertiser is given a layout or script by an advertising agency, the first question therefore is to ask: what is the idea for this advertisement? What is the proposition? Great advertising generally has a great concept.

The Esso tiger has run for many years. As a communications concept, it has sealed off Esso from other petroleum products, and has given it a very clear and singular identity and special quality.

The tiger says power, authority, high performance. It says all this remarkably quickly, at a glance. It is a concept which is utterly relevant to the product category, and which becomes associated with Esso over time. You see a tiger, you think of Esso, you think of power.

The line about Heineken – 'refreshes the parts other beers cannot reach' – has positioned Heineken as a distinctive, front-of-mind product. The beer market is crowded, there are dozens of products and many advertising campaigns. There is also natural consumer confusion about what beer is which, and what advertising is for which beer. Within all this clutter, Heineken is memorable, sociable, amusing and attractive. It is the one you do remember.

The insurance industry has seen the enormous growth of direct, often telephone based, insurance, led by Direct Line. The Direct Line advertising shows an amusing and highly mobile red telephone. The little red phone says – simple, just one call, friendly, without any of those daunting insurance formalities.

Concepts can take many forms. Some are visual, some are verbal, some are serious, some are amusing, some spell it all out and some just imply, some use a demonstration and some a character or personality (such as the Esso Tiger we have mentioned, or Brooke Bond Tea chimpanzees, or the Tango Man). Whatever form they do take, advertising campaigns must begin by trying to obtain or discover a concept. Without a relevant idea or proposition, the campaign will be empty.

A real, workable concept must meet a number of key considerations:

■ Does it communicate a point? What is that point?
■ Does it communicate that point clearly?
■ What does it promise about the product?
■ Is that promise meaningful to the audience?

Above all, a concept must speak in the customer's terms. Superior creativity can only arise from better understanding of the customer, and of speaking from the customer's point of view. Commercial communication has to be customer orientated, rooted in what the customer knows, feels and wants, and talking in the terms and kind of language used by the customer. That is to say, commercial communication is customer communication. The advertiser in a sense represents the customer and the advertising speaks for the customer. It says what the customer may say.

Successful concepts do not repeat product formulae or technical specifications. They make a customer statement.

'Have a break, have a Kit Kat' does not talk about Kit Kat as a chocolate wafer block. The customer regards Kit Kat as a snack, and that is what the advertising concept presents it as.

The popular Nescafé Gold Blend advertising shows the use of coffee in social relationships. That is how people see it.

The father–daughter relationship in the Renault Clio advertising gives the product an air of flexibility, informality and charm. It maximises the value of the manufacturing origin of the car.

So, significant advertising rests on a strong, basic concept. An idea or proposition that summarises what the product stands for, not in advertising speak but in terms of customer outlook. That is what to pursue.

THE OFFER

Central to the creative concept is an offer, or a promise, or a proposition about what the product or service can do for the customer.

It answers an unspoken question: tell me what I get out of this? Or, what is in this product for *me*?

If a product has nothing to offer a customer there is no point in considering it. That is to say, an advertisement must give a customer a *reason to buy*. It can be presented in two forms:

1. Direct, overt, practical, factual. Such as 'It pays to specify JCB'. Or 'BT call charges are reduced' Or 'Selfridges Summer Sale opens Saturday. Enormous savings!'
2. Indirect, implied, emotional, atmospheric. The Häagen-Dazs ice-cream advertising does not *talk* in terms of flavour or product content. But it does show a clear value in the product. The Famous Grouse press advertisement says little in so many words. But its imagery is loaded with signs, of heritage, of tradition, of being long established, of Scottishness.

Some situations lend themselves more to the direct and overt route, others more to the image-laden or subconscious imagery route. Markets, uses, customer impressions will vary and so each campaign will require its own language of persuasion. But, direct or indirect, conscious or subconscious, a clear offer to the reader must emerge.

Above all else, advertisements will offer and sell a benefit. What will this product do? What will it do for me? What will it do for me better than I am getting now?

It could be argued that advertising and product categories split into two basic divisions, each dependent on a kind of market situation:

1. *Consumer goods:* non-essential choices, emotional to a degree, based sometimes on whim.
2. *Business-to-business goods or services:* often decided by professionals. A rational decision for rational purposes, based on a rational process.

Many consumer goods are bought irrationally, and are emotional to a degree. Many professional or capital goods are bought under practical guidelines, and are rational and conscious choices. But buying situations are not always that cut and dried. The business purchaser is still a human being, with human feelings and needs. Consumers with money to spend generally try to spend it wisely and prudently. So, purchasing is often a *mix* of the practical and the emotional, the rational and the subconscious. The emphasis varies, but the mix of reasons remains.

So, the benefit has to reflect this duality.

What does *my* product do for *you*, in terms of what you are looking for? The benefit will be what the customer wants most: superior performance or lower price or greater speed or better service or greater social satisfaction.

Another important factor here is that of 'added value'. The advertisement should try to add value to the product, since customers in advertising terms do not buy physical products but benefits.

In this sphere, my product works better for you. Persil cares for your hands and your clothes as well as making clothes whiter. The advertising and hence the product add value to the basic specification. Martini adds a value of sophistication. BT makes telephoning not just a matter of communication but of an enhanced social life.

So, here the advertiser must ask, what value does my product add, and how far can my advertising express this?

TALKING ABOUT A DIFFERENCE

A further vital element in an advertising concept is its ability to separate the product out from the competition. Most products or services do face or encounter competition of one kind or another. Markets are increasingly competitive and few products are safe.

In addition, many markets are crowded or cluttered and customers may have difficulty in identifying or understanding all the competitors. Within a crowded and competitive market, the customer again will ask an unspoken question: why should I consider *your* product? What do you have to offer in particular? What have you got that the others have not got?

The advertiser will fail to answer that at their peril.

Advertising in consequence increasingly becomes an instrument of product differentation. Of separating the product out, of giving it a different value, of finding for it a product plus.

Concepts sell benefits. And they also sell differences.

Some differences may again be physical. Products can be longer, heavier, quicker, cheaper, better serviced, better engineered, more reliable.

But equally differences may be emotional. Products can confer status, or provide satisfaction, or social acceptability, or be an expression of motherhood, or of self-confidence.

Differences underlie many advertising campaigns, but they must be:

■ relevant to the customer and not just artificial
■ realistic, and borne out by experience: if you overpromise a difference and fail to deliver, you may be in terrible trouble
■ understandable, and not so complicated to express that the audience stops paying attention after five seconds
■ helpful: the difference must be one that does something for the customer; Volvo seeming to be built stronger clearly does – it is both helpful and true to the image of Volvo as it is.

In essence, therefore, an advertising concept:

■ must make a promise or a proposition
■ must offer a benefit
■ should add a value to the product
■ should show a product difference or a product plus.

And it should all be in the language and the mode of behaviour of the market, not the advertiser.

THE FINISHED ADVERTISEMENT

The concept now moves on to a finished advertisement, into words and pictures. Making both these requires creative skill and professional disciplines.

A finished advertisement has a number of basic elements:

- *a headline:* the main announcement
- possibly a *subhead* or series of subheads, heading separate sections
- *body-copy,* or the main text
- *a base line,* commonly used to carry a slogan
- *a logotype,* or company or product name
- *illustration or illustrations:* often a main illustration with secondary illustrations in support
- *product or pack shot,* showing the product appearance and then perhaps
- a *coupon,* to be filled in, for fuller information
- a *telephone number,* to be used to call for information, or a Web Site number
- *an address:* how to contact the company
- *a price:* many advertisements, however, avoid this, and do not quote price. Often, it is not needed.

Poster design is usually much simpler, with a short headline, a bold illustration and little else.

TV commercials contain movement and sound. In particular they have:

- *live action or animation,* for the visual sequences
- *dialogue,* either spoken to camera or a voice-over
- *music and/or sound effects,* sometimes a jingle
- *an end title:* a final summation in words
- *an end shot:* often a product shot.

A strong concept has to be carried through in strong and competent execution. The golden rules for this are a matter of common-sense and practicality.

▉ *Balance:* illustration should not dominate headline and vice versa. The elements must be in balance.

▉ *Brevity:* an advertisement must work quickly. While the length of copy must necessarily vary, advertisements gain from being short, sharp and to the point.

▉ *Simplicity:* clutter and overcomplication must be avoided.

▉ *Readability and viewability:* the finished result should be easy to read or to watch. London Underground tube cards which are impossible to read from a foot away merely annoy the audience and convey nothing.

▉ *Attention getting:* the advertisement must somehow gain the audience's attention, by the strength of the headline, a provocative phrase or unusual visual, a striking design, a strong typography, a dominating proposition.

The advertisement works if it is seen, remembered, and conveys a message with intrinsic value. That is what makes it 'creative'.

ADVERTISEMENT CHECKLIST

▪ What does this advertisement offer?
▪ What does it promise the audience?
▪ Is this promise relevant – helpful – understandable?
▪ What benefit does the product offer?
▪ Is it clear, understandable, of value to the customer?

▪ Does the advertisement give a difference to the product?
▪ Or an advantage, or superiority?
▪ Is there a strong slogan or main claim?

▪ Looking at the advertisement:
  – Can I see it clearly?
  – Are all the words legible and easy to follow?
  – Or are the soundtrack and visual easy to comprehend?
  – Does it have a strong headline?
  – Does it make it plain what the product is?
  – Is the body-copy easy to understand?
  – Is the body-copy persuasive?
  – Does the product or service name stand out clearly?
  – Is there a compelling illustration?
  – Is there a sufficient demonstration of the product?
  – Are all the basic facts conveyed?
  – Is there a good enough pack shot or product shot?
  – Does the style conform to corporate guidelines?
  – Is there a telephone number or address? Are they legible?
  – Do I need a Web number?
  – Does it contain a 'next action', or suggest what the audience does now?
  – How fast does the advertisement work? Is it too long?

▪ Trying to protect myself:
  – Is there anything here that should not be?
  – Are all the claims sustainable?
  – Is it all legal?

▪ Does the whole effect, in image terms, conform to the general image and standing of the advertiser?

▪ How far does the advertisement carry on from and have continuity elements from previous advertising?

7

Practical Advertisement Production

HOW TO PRODUCE AN ADVERTISEMENT

Once a media space is selected, and once the advertisement copy has been decided, it is necessary to convert that message into a final production form to fill that space.

All the media organisations will supply is the space. The advertiser must supply the finished advertisement material.

Most media do, however, offer production facilities. The advertiser can, if necessary, book the space, conceive the basic message and then get it produced into artwork by the media themselves.

Newspapers, TV and radio operate editorial divisions with full production facilities and will offer basic production capabilities as part of their service to the advertiser.

Therefore, in many circumstances advertisers do use media for advertisement production. Nevertheless, it is true to say that the bulk of advertisement production is either handled directly by the advertiser or by the advertising agency retained by the advertiser.

The benefits of using the media are varied:

■ production can be quick and cheap
■ it is simpler to use one source for placing space and for filling it
■ the media may have specialist skills tailored to the particular medium in which they operate.

But there are a range of limitations:

■ Advertisement production is not the primary task of the media.
■ They may not have as high a level of advertisement skills as an advertising agency.
■ They do not have the background and familiarity with the product that an advertising agency may have.
■ The media may not have as much time to devote to the job as an agency will need to have. Indeed, the media would prefer not to devote an undue amount of staff time to low-income projects.
■ Advertisements produced direct by the media often tend to be simple, basic and unsophisticated. Values which are helpful for some advertisements (eg for sales announcements) but not sufficient when quality and sophistication are vital.

The advertiser must therefore choose the *method* for producing an advertisement – doing it himself, using the facilities of the advertising medium or using a fully-fledged advertising agency.

Occasions for asking a media representative to help could include the following:

■ When the advertiser does not have an agency and none is available.
■ When the advertisement is one-off. Many agencies do not handle one-off jobs, whereas the media are happy to do this.
■ Where the advertisement is extremely simple.
■ Where the budget is very limited. For example, radio stations can produce rough commercials at a very low cost, using their own internal studio facilities. The price is often nominal.
■ Where there is very little time.

In certain categories, the media will by definition do the production. Classified advertising is set by the newspaper. Magazines and newspapers will do the production for advertorials or for editorial features. This is often the value of such features. They seem to be part of the general editorial of the publication.

Again, at the most basic level an advertisement may not need to be 'produced' at all. In newspapers or magazines it may be paper set. That is, the publication will typeset it as part of its normal typesetting process. This is satisfactory where the advertisement is all text. It does not work where an illustration is required, or where the advertisement requires its own special style separate from that of the publication.

For this reason, paper setting of advertisements is very limited in its use and is not widely practised.

When the advertiser decides that there are valid grounds (such as money or time) they may therefore use the medium:

■ either to paper set the advertisement
■ or to carry out full production.

But when a more developed or personalised advertisement is needed (which is a matter for judgement) then the advertiser may either do it himself – or use an advertising agency.

Internal or self-produced advertisements are growing in extent. It is not *always* necessary to use an advertising agency.

There are two ways in which production can be carried out directly by an advertiser.

1. The advertiser may produce the text and use an outside studio to do the production, ie an outside supplier with production equipment. Among outside suppliers who can be called on are:
   – quick-print shops, which generally offer a service for type-setting and artwork
   – typing or secretarial bureaux, which may use a word-processor or computer capable of producing simple artwork
   – a local graphics studio. Many areas may possess a studio or designer, servicing retailers, architects, builders etc, who can also produce finished artwork for advertisers.
   Here again, results may often be simple and uncomplex, quick and cheap. In many cases this is enough. In many cases, it is not.
2. An increasing number of organisations possess their own in-house equipment, eg computer or wordprocessor with a graphics package. These may not primarily be used for advertising purposes but certainly can produce a reasonable standard of advertisement artwork if so required. Indeed, they have become commonplace. Once more, the result may be simple and straightforward, and of all methods is the fastest and cheapest. But again, the result may lack quality, and may not be satisfactory when a higher level of finish or of creative originality is needed. At which point, the standard advertising agency may be necessary – and often is – to provide the expertise, the skill and the creativity required for major-level advertising campaigns.

Therefore, it is important for an advertiser to decide on the *method* of producing an advertisement before embarking on the production itself, and a rough set of guidelines therefore emerges:

- for classified advertisements, paper setting
- for very simple and brief announcements, paper setting
- for advertorials and editorial features, production by the media themselves
- for simple, quick and cheap production, use of the media
- for simple, direct and low-cost production, use of the advertiser's own internal equipment, if this is available
- for simple, text-based production, use of a secretarial bureau
- for slightly more complex effects, use of a quick-print shop
- for more developed visuals and higher level of finish, use of a local studio or designer.

On the whole the above methods are sensible when production is occasional, the budget low, the time limited and the use small scale.

But when the advertising is considerable, the budget larger, the timing ongoing and the campaign requirement complex, then the conventional advertising agency, or the larger commercial studio, is usually needed.

Finally, it should also be said that certain specialist suppliers of specialist services can, and do willingly, offer a production service. Two examples of such specialist service are:

1. *Direct mail.* The direct mail house provides a design, writing and production facility as well as fulfilment. Indeed, many users of direct mail prefer to use the direct mail house for production rather than anyone else, on grounds of expertise and economy. Thus, the advertiser may retain an advertising agency to produce mainstream media advertisements, but also retain a direct mail house for mailing production.
2. *Print and literature.* The larger printers will commonly operate a studio, offering specialist print design so that they can carry out a combined package of design and production, again with expertise and specialist skill.

PRESS PRODUCTION

Newspapers and magazines require the advertiser to supply the advertisement material. This can be supplied in one of three ways:

1. by providing original artwork from which the publication can print
2. by providing duplicates of the original artwork
3. by inputting the artwork down the line by electronic means directly into the publisher's printing process, ie via ISDN or ADS.

Where a booking is made in one publication only, the original artwork may be used. This saves the cost of a duplicate, and may produce a slightly better effect. On the other hand, there is the danger that the artwork might get damaged or lost and so it is safer to provide duplicates. Where there are a number of media bookings then it becomes inevitable that duplicates will be required. Duplicates must be supplied on special stock, satisfactory for reproduction purposes.

But it is likely that electronic transmission of artwork, particularly colour artwork, will become standard practice. ISDN is expanding and will soon become the norm. This is a digital system that allows fast, simple use of transmission on-line.

Black and white advertisements

Advertisements consist of two elements:

1. word, or text
2. pictures.

Both need to be produced into artwork form.

Text

The wording must be typeset. This can be done using a specialist typesetter, or by using typesetting equipment operated within a studio. The days of former 'hot metal' typesetting are over, and type is now generally set by computer, with a specialist typesetting software program.

The type is run off as a proof, which must be read and corrected. Or it can be printed out as part of a composite text and illustration proof. Where the text is simple and short, the latter probably saves time and money. Where the text is long and complex, the advertiser may be better advised to see a separate proof of the typesetting alone.

The proof will need to be examined closely for accuracy, for the suitability of the typefaces, and for the clarity of type size.

Graphic elements

Most advertisements will contain a variety of graphic elements. These include not only a main illustration or illustrations but other important graphic constituents – such as the company or brand logotype, a corporate symbol or a product illustration.

Ongoing elements such as logotypes may be scanned into the computer and kept on file for future use and reuse.

A combined text and graphics proof needs to be seen, and again must be examined closely:

■ for the best balance of illustration against text
■ for the clarity and reproduction quality of the illustration
■ for the standard of subsidiary graphics such as logotypes, product shots, location diagrams etc.

The final advertisement can then be sent off to the publication. Where duplicates are required, they will be needed in one of two forms:

1. *For line illustrations or simple text.* Here duplicates can be supplied either as PMTs or as bromides. But many computer printers can produce a satisfactory enough result for reproduction purposes on a cheaper material such as Mellotex.
2. *For half-tone illustrations* the advertiser or agency may need to supply film. Simple line drawings do not require half-tone. But photographs do. The tonal values are too graduated for line reproduction. The half-tone process can reproduce this gradation by breaking the image down into a fine network of small dots, via a half-tone screen. Here, the publication will require film, which is substantially more expensive than bromides or Mellotex.

Colour advertisements

Magazines (and newspapers too, where they run colour spaces) will require colour artwork.

Here, too, the advertiser or agency may provide original artwork where there is only one booking, or duplicates where there are many.

The original artwork must be clear and unambiguous since the colour process is an expensive one and mistakes must be avoided.

Advertisement colour printing is usually done out of four basic colours – black, magenta, cyan (blue) and yellow. These will combine in printing to form a full colour effect. However, if a special colour is required, then it may be necessary to add that special colour on to the basic four colours: to go to five colours, or perhaps six. Examples here are special logotype colours, company house colours, special product colours. Here it will be necessary to check with the publication to ensure that five or six-colour printing is acceptable.

Original artwork needs to be delivered in the following form:

■ a board containing the (black and white) text plus a guide to the illustration
■ the illustration in the form of a transparency
■ a masking on the outside of the transparency to indicate which areas of the illustration are to be printed
■ a written colour guide and instruction.

Where duplicates are required for a range of bookings, colour film must be supplied. This can be extremely expensive, and costs must be kept under control. Colour separations are produced in film form, separating the image out into its basic colours.

It is vital to see a colour proof, arising from the colour separations, to check for accuracy and for colour quality. The most common form of proof is that of the cromalin or match print.

Where an amendment is required, a second colour proof should be seen. Time is often a problem and therefore, in colour work, some days should be built in for the production of satisfactory proofs.

Once the material has been sent to the publication it too should submit a colour proof, showing the colour effect within its own printing process. Again, amendments and improvements may be called for. And, again, sufficient time must be allowed.

The improving prevalence of electronic transmission – ISDN or ADS – will cut the time involved and possibly the cost, although ISDN costs can be higher than expected.

POSTER PRODUCTION

Posters contractors only supply space on their hoardings. So here again the agency or advertiser must supply final printed posters, to size. This goes through two processes:

1. production of the original artwork
2. poster printing.

There are various methods of simulating a colour proof. From a small-scale printed version, to projection on to a screen, to use of a light-box. But there is no substitute for seeing a full-scale version, pasted up *in situ* on to a poster site.

Poster printing is one of the most costly areas of advertising production, since separate posters are required for each site plus spares. Considerable attention therefore needs to be paid to obtaining competitive printing quotations from specialist poster printers.

PRINT AND LITERATURE PRODUCTION

This follows roughly the same process as press and posters, namely:

■ development of original artwork
■ printing by a specialist printer.

The agency or advertiser will produce the original artwork in the same form as for colour press:

■ typesetting
■ indicated illustration areas
■ transparencies for illustrations, marked-up for printing
■ other flat artwork
■ colour and printing instructions.

The printer will then produce a colour proof. This can take one of three forms:

1. a cromalin
2. a set of running sheets, ie printed sheets, on the paper required
3. full paper proofs, on the paper required, trimmed and cut to size.

The cost will vary for these stages of proof. The more elaborate, the more expensive. These proofs must be carefully checked for quality and colour values.

TV PRODUCTION

TV is far more complex as a medium, and far more complex for advertising production purposes than press or posters. It is also far more costly. Indeed, TV production is considerably the most expensive area of advertisement production and has been subject to enormous cost inflation in the past ten years. While this may have levelled off, it is a subject where the advertiser must take great care. Only those with substantial funds and with adequate control mechanisms should venture into it. Revisions and extra shooting add to the expense – so TV production has to be *right*, from the start. Here again, the advertiser may take one of three courses:

Use of a TV station's own production facilities
This can make for cheaper production, in a simpler and quicker way. But it is less satisfactory for more elaborate production jobs or those used extensively by time or by region.

Local advertisers, limited offers, sales announcements, special events or special promotions may best use this resource.

Direct use of specialist TV commercials production company
Most commercials are in practice produced by specialist production houses. Advertisers can use them direct if they wish, and many do. It cuts out the middleperson ie the advertising agency, can save on agency mark-ups, and can save on time.

However this is an area where considerable experience is vital, and the advertiser may find an advertising agency indispensable, in providing expertise, coordination and TV skills of its own. If the agency has also been used to conceive the original TV commercial script, it may be prudent to let it see the whole job through from inception into the production stage.

Nevertheless direct use of production companies is an option to be considered.

Use of an advertising agency
The agency can supply considerable supervising skills, and save the client time – and overheads. It is sometimes a question of how well and extensively staffed is the client. A large volume of commercials is made through agencies, for reasons of practicality and through commonsense.

Stages of TV commercial production

Commercials may take longer to produce than any other form of advertising, though they can be rushed through quickly if needed. They go through a series of stages usually broken down into pre-production, production and post-production.

1. Agreement of script.
2. Selection of a production company. Usually on the basis of comparative costings.
3. Agreement of a production costing.
4. Casting. Done from a selection of talent.
5. Music. Commissioned from a specialist composer. Here, too, there are several stages:
   - writing the score
   - production of a pilot track
   - studio recording of final track – this will involve hiring a studio, a group of musicians or an orchestra, and the use of a singer or a group of singers.
6. Pre-production. A director will be commissioned, and necessary elements will be agreed in advance, including costumes and set design. The general nature of the shoot will be agreed.
7. Filming. This will involve:
   - hiring a film studio, or finding a suitable location
   - assembling a crew of different film specialists.
   Filming may take several days.
8. Post-production. This will involve dubbing, adding sound effects or special effects etc.
9. Soundtrack. If a voice-over is required, this will be done in a separate recording. Again, various elements are involved:
   - casting the voice, out of a range of possible voices
   - sometimes producing a pilot-track
   - hiring a studio, and operating a recording session.
10. Editing. Where all the various elements are put together.
11. The client will then see a film of the edited version.
12. Amendments can be made, to cutting, dubbing etc.
13. Once the commercial is agreed, sets of videos are sent out to the TV stations (who will charge a handling charge).

It should be noted that all TV commercials need to go through an agreement process with the TV system itself. Commercials must be cleared in advance before they can be transmitted:

■ in script form
■ in produced film form.

RADIO PRODUCTION

Radio commercial production echoes that of TV production, though it is much cheaper, and far simpler. Again, it consists of a number of stages:

1. Agreement of script.
2. Selection of a commercials' production house, or use of a radio station.
3. Selection of producer.
4. Casting of a voice or voices.
5. Commissioning of music, with the commissioning of a composer, production of a pilot-track, full recording, etc.
   Alternatively, library music may be used. Many radio commercials use library music, which is quicker, cheaper and less complicated.
6. Recording session, with the hire of a studio.
7. Playback to the client and agreement.
8. Distribution of tapes to the various radio stations.

COST CONTROL

Advertisement production can be the cause of much anxiety, and large amounts of money may be at risk. Cost-control guidelines therefore need to be firm and unmistakable. We will be examining methods of cost control in greater detail in the next chapter but at this point certain basic principles need to be emphasised. They are a matter of commonsense and sound practice.

The use of reliable suppliers
Most advertisement production is carried out through a wide range of suppliers. Over time, the advertiser must identify those which are reliable, responsible and economic.

Agreement of a budget in advance
This is easier to do with large jobs than with small. A TV

commercial may (indeed must) be costed carefully at an early stage. But it is far more difficult to assess in advance the cost of a small press advertisement done overnight in a rush. Nevertheless, guidelines can apply here, too.

Comparative, competitive quotations

Large production jobs (eg poster printing, leaflets, TV commercials) need to go out for competitive tendering. A standard brief must, of course, be used for this purpose.

The correct technique

The best, and most economic, technique needs to be employed for the particular job. There is a wide variety of possible techniques available in most cases. It is important to decide which is the right one to use, at the planning stage. Sensible planning saves money afterwards.

Control of timing

The greater the rush, the greater the cost.

TIMING

Timing is the essence of advertisement production.

The new technology has generally reduced time and enables jobs to be done more speedily. But it is still vital to allow enough time:

■ to ensure good enough quality
■ to avoid undue cost.

Different media require different timings, but the following should provide a rough guideline as to sensible requirements. They are *minima*.

Press production: black and white

■ Allow two weeks for photography, to book a photographer, a studio and a model and to design and build sets. For star models or photographers well over two weeks may be needed.
■ Prints or photographs: 24 hours, or less.
■ Typesetting: overnight is possible, but allow 24 hours.

■ Complete proof of full artwork: three to five days, depending on complexity.
■ Revisions of proofs: 24 to 48 hours.
■ Duplicates: bromides etc can be produced within half a day.
■ Black and white film: 24 hours.

Press production: colour

■ Colour separations and colour proofs: three days, but four preferable.
■ Revisions to colour proofs: 48 hours.
■ Colour film: allow three days, but two possible. Overnight is often required, but is not desirable.

It must be said that things are getting shorter all the time, and the production process is continually speeding up, but often at the expense of quality and economy.

Poster production

■ Proof of poster: 14 days.
■ Delivery of full run: up to four weeks, depending on size of the run.

Print and literature production

This will vary according to the nature of the job, quality, materials, size of the printed surface, among other things. For a medium-sized job, in four colours, using simple artwork, a cromalin can be obtained in a week or less.

Delivery of the full production run will vary according to the nature of the job but for an average middle-of-the-road job 14 days should be allowed from approval of proof, to include finishing. Certain extras such as varnishing may require longer.

TV production

In view of the elaborate nature of the production process, allow eight weeks. Complex production may require much longer.

Radio production

■ A local station can produce a commercial in three to four days.

■ For commercial production, allow two weeks for a simple commercial.
■ A more elaborate commercial, or one with commissioned music, may take some weeks more. A major commercial may take six weeks.

In emergency circumstances, the above timings may well be improved. It is possible to do things within hours, not days. But producing needs thinking time as well as doing time, and panic timings can lead to errors as well as high overtime charges.

QUALITY CONTROL

Many advertisers are disappointed with their results. The finished effect may be less than expected. Production standards will make or mar an advertising campaign. Quality guidelines are as vital as cost guidelines, if not more so. The advertiser/client must exercise control throughout.

Concept stage
The production implications need to be examined and fully agreed at the time when the advertising concept is formulated. This will avoid misunderstanding later. High-quality reproduction must spring from what is to be produced.

Suppliers
The supplier must match the quality required. In many cases, a moderate job will not need above average suppliers. The choice of the supplier-photographer, printer, typesetter will determine the quality level obtained.

Expenditure
It does not *always* follow that quality costs more. But a cut-price budget is unlikely to obtain the highest quality, if quality is the requisite. Thus, in competitive estimates, the lowest quote does not always win.

Reference to the original
The client should always refer back to the original – script or design – to ensure that production matches the original agreed concept.

Time to amend

The timetable *must* allow time for proper proofing, revision, improvement and reproofing. Amendments are usually necessary and must be allowed for.

Agreement

All concerned should agree the job before it is finalised. Committees should be avoided, but the client should be included in all critical stages of advertisement production.

Standard

In some cases, it is possible for certain standards to be laid down and quality of reproduction can be checked against them. For example, a precise colour (a pantone number) for the company logotype or symbol, a size or manner of handling for the logotype or product illustration.

Media fit

Reproduction should match the medium and should be seen in the context of the medium. For example, press proofs should be pasted in to newspaper pages, TV films shown within a reel of commercials. Quality can only be judged within the environment in which the job is to appear.

PRODUCTION CHECKLIST

Choice of suppliers   Costing   Timetable

Press, print, posters
Typesetting
Photography
Artwork
Proof
Amended proof
Type of duplicate
Number of duplicates
ISDN or ADS
Delivery

TV
Selection of production company
Selection of director
Casting
Costume design
Set design
Location search
Music – composers
       – pilot track
       – full recording
Pre-production meeting
Filming – studio
        – crew
Recording voice-track
Editing
Post-production
View film
View amended film
Delivery

Radio
Selection of production company
Selection of producer
Casting
Music – library
       – commission composer
       – full recording
Recording – studio
Playback to client
Recorded playback
Delivery of tapes

8

The Budget and the Plan

THE FINANCIAL IMPERATIVE

Advertising represents an expenditure of money. It is a way of spending part of the organisation's finances and, in financial terms, is no different in essence from any other way of committing corporate expenditure. The organisation undertakes spending because it has to and in order to obtain a return. Therefore it judges the expenditure in terms of value and in terms of the worth of the results.

Most organisations are governed by their financial position and by the financial guidelines and controls that are set. Advertising is as much subject to these controls as any other activity.

The questions that have to be asked therefore are: is this expenditure justified, do we have to make it, do we have to make it now, does it represent value for money and will we be getting back a value in proportion to the size of the expenditure?

Indeed, advertising may be regarded as an investment which might be compared to other possible and rival investments. Which is better now? To spend £10,000 on advertising, or to spend it on a new computer system, or to spend it on a general programme of staff training? They are all claims to corporate finances, and advertising has to justify itself against other ways of spending the money, just as much as any expenditure must do.

In practice, departments have their own budgets and organisations try not to let one department take from another. But the advertising budget is not sacrosanct and has to be handled scrupulously. It is not there to produce pretty pictures or give everyone a jolly time, and is continuously subject to management accountability and financial control.

At the back of their mind, therefore, the advertiser must always be asking: is this a worthwhile expenditure and am I getting value for money?

FORMING A BUDGET

Most organisations operate by budget and usually by an annual budget per department. Those departments which conduct advertising will therefore normally carry a general annual budget. All the advertising budget might go through one department, or be spread if several departments conduct their own separate advertising programmes. For example:

■ *Situation one:* communications department – total budget for all advertising
■ *Situation two:* marketing department – budget for marketing communications; personnel department – budget for recruitment advertising; corporate relations department – budget for corporate advertising.

It is more usual for organisations to consolidate their advertising budgets where possible, for reasons of control or better coordination. But it is a decision that has to be made by the management and ultimately by the board of directors. The size of expenditure and the width of activities will be the determining factors.

The major part of the budget will be for marketing purposes or for corporate purposes in the case of non-commercial organisations.

A key decision is precisely how to form a budget. What will be the basis for developing one?

Some organisations may not budget at all but proceed on a need-to-spend basis. If an advertisement has to run, let it run. If we think an advertisement is necessary, let us try it out and see what happens. Smaller businesses or sole proprietors might proceed in this way. They have no need to report to anyone else, so might not bother. But even here, the merits of operating a formal, structured budget are considerable. It is valuable for accounting purposes, it is necessary for financial control, and it will relate advertising to other expenditures in the interest of profitability and calculating a surplus.

Budgeting is an indispensable part of the process of forecasting a profit and of profit and loss control. It is equally so for everyone. Therefore, organisations need to budget. So they need to decide on the basis for achieving an advertising budget, which is often one of their largest forms of expenditure. There are a number of systems which may be adopted.

The task method

I think I need a certain advertising job to be done. To do it properly will cost me a certain sum. I have calculated it precisely and that will be the advertising budget.

This has the merit of providing a worthwhile sum to do an effective job. But it suffers from the overriding flaw of not being related to outcome or to what the expenditure can achieve – or what the organisation can afford.

A percentage of sales

This is the most usual method. A survey conducted by an industrial publisher into industrial and business-to-business advertisers revealed that over 80 per cent ran their advertising budgets on this system. It can work in two ways:

1. as a percentage of this year's forecast sales revenue
2. as a percentage of last year's actual sales revenue.

In practice, most organisations adopt the first of these, since it is related to what the advertising may achieve currently. A percentage of the forecast sales for the year is allocated to advertising purposes, or to marketing and communications purposes in general. This relates expenditure to sales and from that to income. If the sales are achieved, advertising will have been in balance with income and so a profit will have been made. From this point of view, advertising is seen as a prime cost of selling.

The crucial question here is: what percentage? How much is to be allocated? In practice, the organisation will factor out all its basic costs and will try to achieve a balance between them. The advertising budget will be set against the other forms of expenditure, and a reasonable percentage will emerge, hopefully for all of them.

A deciding factor here will be the salience or the importance of the advertising effort. It is partly a question of the needs of the product and partly a factor of the market or product category as a whole. Some markets have a high need for advertising and some a low need. Taking two examples:

1. *The bread market.* This is largely a commodity market. There is little branding. But there is some branding or communication requirement. We will allocate 1 per cent.
2. *The perfume market.* We sell images. We are dependent on how we project ourselves and on the sophisticated identity we can create. We absolutely need to advertise. It is our lifeblood. We will allocate 30 per cent of sales revenue.

The more the market is a commodity, the lower the percentage. The more it is image or advertising dependent, the higher the spend.

In relation to our competitors
The advertiser needs to offset competition and to stand out against it. Therefore, it is wise to spend in proportion to what the competitors or at least the market spends. This may be done in two ways:

1. My major competitor spends £X. I am the same size. I need to spend £X.
2. The market as a whole spends £Y on advertising. I represent 20 per cent of the market, therefore I need to spend 20 per cent of £Y.

This approach has the merit of matching the competition in an increasingly competitive environment. It is crucial to take competition into account. But it is not related to profitability or anticipated sales volume and also suffers from the flaw of needing to find out what the competition or the market are actually now spending. This is often very difficult to do.

However, it is a fact that there is a relationship between share of market and share of market expenditure. This cannot be ignored. If the market is volatile and subject to massive, competitive activity it may be necessary to spend up either to protect the present sales situation or to attack the competitors before they attack the company.

As a percentage of the overheads and the profit

There are certain costs a company has to undertake. These are the fixed and variable costs of production and distribution. Such costs include plant and machinery, factory staff, raw materials, costs of delivery and cost of premises. Advertising is not a fixed cost. Organisations do not absolutely need to advertise as part of the production process. What is left over after removing the fixed costs is a surplus, which can go totally to profit or may be diverted partially to advertising.

While this may be correct from an accountancy point of view, it does not relate to the market or to sales or income and is a generally negative way of formulating an advertising budget.

The case rate method

Where the company sells individual units, a kind of mini-budget can be ascribed to each unit. These units may be sold by the case (a case of soap or a case of biscuits) and the case is factored into prime costs of production and distribution with an element or percentage ascribed to advertising. If a case or unit of 24 packets selling at 65p each fetches £15.60, a percentage is allowed to advertising, say 12 per cent. This means that the unit carries an advertising factor of around £1.87. If a volume of one million cases is forecast then an advertising budget of £1,870,000 emerges. As sales proceed, if more cases get sold the advertising expenditure goes up, if sales decline then the expenditure goes down. All units produce their own spending, and there is an absolute relation to sales.

This is an ingenious way of reaching a precise balance between expenditure and sales, but suffers from the possible difficulty of constantly adjusting the advertising schedule in line with rising or falling sales.

It also can only operate when the notion of cases or units is relevant.

A model of expenditure

In an age of high technology, many organisations have tried to use modern techniques to develop a more precise, or optimal budget pattern. They have used computer simulation models or operational research approaches. In theory, a technique that can factor in all variables and produce a structured statistical response should be of great potential value. In practice, however, few companies have formed a satisfactory formula or have been willing to risk their fortunes on theoretical models.

A TOTAL BUDGET

It should be emphasised that budgets produced are usually total budgets for communications as a whole, rather than purely advertising budgets. So the percentage of forecast turnover approach will produce an overall budget; that is, a total marketing communications budget. This will cover all necessary ingredients: advertising, direct mail, literature, exhibitions, display material and so on.

What is included in the budget?

In particular, does the budget also contain the two important factors of public relations and sales promotion? In addition to pure media advertising, many companies also operate large programmes for PR and for sales promotion. Should these be separate budgets? In practice, most organisations with a commercial need see themselves running a total budget for marketing purposes. This will cover all needs – advertising, public relations, sales promotion, telemarketing and so on – that is, wherever there is a marketing purpose. The implication here is that certain items of expenditure such as public relations might come under several headings or spending departments. As an example:

▓ marketing department: advertising, sales promotion, product PR
▓ corporate affairs department: corporate and public affairs PR.

But generally, for smaller organisations, one consolidated communications budget covers all headings and all needs.

Organisations think and plan in terms of integrated marketing communications. This increasingly will mean one integrated budget.

How is the budget to be split?

Dividing a budget up is a matter of judgement and will be carefully negotiated between all the parties concerned. A common stance in marketing organisations is to split the budget between two main categories, commonly labelled 'above the line' and 'below the line'.

In essence, above the line will cover those elements relating to the media of communication and to persuasion and publicity, while below the line will cover sales promotion, incentives and those methods bearing upon inducing sales. Often, the determining division is between those activities remunerated out of media commissions and those activities paid by fee.

above the line	A	or	B
	advertising		advertising
	direct mail		
	literature		
	PR etc		
below the line	Sales promotion		Direct mail, literature etc
	Sales aids		PR

Exhibitions may go either way, but are often placed as below the line. However, many organisations ignore this distinction and just have one total budget, without complication, which may then be split down by activity.

The two largest expenditures are commonly media advertising and sales promotion. Allocating resources between the two is usually a matter of balancing out the needs and reaching a compromise.

The major questions to be faced are, where is the matter of utmost urgency, what is the primary need in the period ahead and where must be the priority? It is probably fair to observe that in a period of recession or market decline or distributor dominance or uncertain sales volume, advertising budgets may be reduced to the benefit of sales promotion. The converse may be true in periods of expansion or market steadiness.

CONTROLLING THE BUDGET

The cardinal sin in advertising management is to exceed the budget, especially by accident. Organisations have gone bankrupt as a result.

The task of the advertiser is to keep advertising expenditure precisely in line with the budget agreed. There are therefore two factors:

1. agreeing a budget, and then allocating it into categories of spending
2. controlling each item of expenditure.

ADVERTISING BUDGET SUMMARY

Product_____   Financial year _____

Summary as at_____(end month)

	Annual Budget		J	F	M	A	M	J	J	A	S	O	N	D
Media advertising Media production Literature Direct mail Exhibitions Audio-visuals Public relations fee Public relations costs Sales aids miscellaneous	B	A	BA	BA										
TOTAL														

Figure 8.1 *Advertising budget summary*

The advertiser has two tools for this: a forward set of budget allocations and expenditure estimates, and a running series of invoices and monthly totals of actual expenditures. The finance or accounts department must supply the advertising manager with clear totals at the end of each month.

There are three control mechanisms which are common.

The first is to maintain a continuing estimate of what has been budgeted and what has been spent. A typical format is shown in Figure 8.1. B stands for budget, A for actual. Budgets are split by activity and by month. As the year progresses, so the actuals are shown against the original budgets.

A second control document reveals what money has been committed and so cannot be cancelled. The difficulty often is not so much actual current spending as what has been committed forward and so which cannot be escaped. A typical control document is shown in Figure 8.2.

A third key control is the provision by the accounts department of a monthly listing of what has been invoiced that month, broken down by supplier, type of supply and cost.

Given these controls, a correct expenditure balance should be maintained throughout the year, with particular attention devoted to the final period.

ADVERTISING COMMITMENT SUMMARY

Product_____   Financial year _____

Summary as at_____(end month)

	Budget for year	Spent to date	Committed	Non-committed
Media advertising Media production Literature Direct mail Exhibitions Audio-visuals etc.				
TOTAL				

Figure 8.2   *Advertising commitment summary*

Cost control

Budgets consist of a multitude of separate costs. Each one needs to be individually evaluated and controlled. To do this, a formal process needs to be followed.

Stage one: an estimate has to be provided and agreed
Whatever the supplier, an estimate must be given for that job. The advertising agency produces a draft schedule or media plan. The photographer produces an estimate for a day's shoot. A printer produces an estimate for 10,000 leaflets.

The estimate should be in writing and must be given formal approval.

Stage two: delivery of job
The job should be produced and delivered, and should be to the advertiser's satisfaction.

Stage three: supplier's invoice
This should be checked against the original estimate, with a proof of delivery – sample of leaflet, voucher copy of press advertisement, certificate of transmission for TV commercial – whatever possible.

Stage four: approval of invoice
This must be checked through the accounts department and then approved or signed off by the advertiser or originating executive.

Stage five: payment
This is made only when the invoice is accepted, and the job approved.

Sub-costs and constituent elements

It should be noted that many types of communication jobs do not consist of one consolidated cost, but of a variety of separate and different costs. This reflects the fact that communications is broken down into a wide set of sub-activities all building up into a totality. It is therefore crucial, in obtaining a costing, to break an overall cost down into its constituent elements and to have an estimate for each.

Two examples of such sub-costs are shown below.

Photography preparation
Photography fee
Model fees
Location
Studio hire
Model making
Casting fees
Home economist
Stylist
Make-up
Hairdresser
Wardrobe
Props
Set design and construction
Film processing
Transport
Lighting hire
Hotels etc

Retouching
Computer retouching
Transparency retouching
Duplicate transparencies
Photo-comps
Colour prints
Black and white prints

Not all of these may be required in any one job. But many may be. It is therefore vital to ask the supplier in any situation to break down a job into its parts, and to provide a cost for each element.

It must also be established that these are final costs, with no extra to come leaking in over the next few weeks.

HOW TO OBTAIN VALUE

The advertiser seeks to get best value for money. The problem here is to decide what best value may be. It is very much a matter of judgement, and there is always the temptation to feel that better value somehow lies somewhere round the next bend.

The pursuit of value is desirable, but needs to be balanced by commonsense. To begin, it is helpful to define what 'value' may be.

It does not necessarily mean cheap. Value for money can come in a variety of guises:

■ lower price
■ higher quality
■ better service
■ faster delivery
■ extras, at no extra charge.

It is always helpful to compare the price with market prices or with average prices prevailing in the industry. Here the advertiser needs experience, or a friendly supplier or colleague to give some comparative information.

There are two major cost categories: media costs and production costs. Value for these can be approached separately.

Media costs

Theoretically, media have rate card rates and value will come about through seeing how far actual rates can be achieved below rate card rates, by means of vigorous negotiation. Some media will negotiate lower rates and some media will allow discounts on the rate card.

But not all media will negotiate price. In exhibitions, exhibition organisers will keep to basic stand costs. The Post Office will allow some rebates on mailing, but will generally not cut postage costs.

Not everyone will agree to deals. But value can still be sought, through such things as better positions, better days of the week, premium spaces at run-of-paper prices and so on. Value means a better product and not just a lower price.

Production costs

It is common practice to obtain competitive estimates for major production work – photography, printing, exhibition stands, corporate design and so on. Often at least three estimates are obtained, for price comparison. This means going to reasonable suppliers in the first place. Three expensive photographers will still mean an expensive photograph.

The rule is to match the level of the supplier with the level of the job in hand. A major job may require a top-grade production company. A more minor job could go to a moderate supplier.

That is why advertisers often may keep a library of two sorts of supplier. The top supplier for top grade jobs. The small person round the corner for incidental, faster or cheaper jobs.

Negotiation

The advertiser needs to negotiate hard, and to debate price with each supplier. It is a constant process.

Subcontractors

Often a contractor is used who brings in subcontractors. The principal example here is advertising agencies. The agency will often need to use an outside supplier itself to help do a job: photographers, printers, colour process houses and so on.

In this case, the advertiser must make it plain to the agency that they expect rigorous cost control of subcontractors.

The advertiser will ask for examples of the subcontractor's work, and will want to know what the pricing levels are. At times, the advertiser may want to see the subcontractor's invoices as well as those of the agency.

In an inflationary period in particular, the quest for value is ceaseless.

PLANNING THE TIMING

Central to the budgeting and cost process is the subject of timing. If the advertiser can control the time, then they can control the costs.

Much, and perhaps most, advertising activity is carried out at the last moment – amid panic. The result is overtime charges, emergency payments and heartache when the invoices arrive.

The art of the communications manager, therefore, is to set timetables, to keep all those involved to the timetable and so avoid last-minute excess charges.

This covers advertisement development as well as production. A typical campaign timetable format is shown in the box.

	Date
Agree outline budget	
Agree strategy	
Submit copy and layout	
Agree copy and layout	
Proceed to photography	
Submit photography	
Agree photography	
Submit advertisement proof	
Agree advertisement proof	
Copy date	

Ideally, overall campaigns are agreed in outline some months before the start of a campaign, and individual advertisements well before a copy date. The advertiser needs to work a timetable out from the structure of copy dates, and allow at least a week between completion and copy date, if at all possible. This is a luxury that is not always practical. In addition, time should be allowed for revisions and amendments.

COMBINED COMMUNICATIONS

Considerations of value and budget control apply to all elements of the marketing communications mix. The ideal is for the advertiser to attain a mix of activities which jointly yield high value for money.

Here, it is necessary to equate value in one form with value in another. This is not always possible. Comparing a 10,000 run leaflet with a poster site is difficult. All the advertiser can do is to follow a reasonable split between types of activity, try to buy each one as well as possible and check on the value obtained in each.

Combined communication is inescapable. The advertiser has to follow a mix of activities as is best required for any particular circumstance. Value goes across them all. The ultimate value is to obtain the highest combined effect at the given budget.

BUDGET CHECKLIST

■ Do you have a budget system?
■ Who produces the data?
■ Who approves budgets?
■ Who authorises expenditures? What system is there?
■ Who approves invoices and authorises payment?
■ How is the budget broken down:
  - by category?
  - by item in that category?
  - by month or period?
■ What is the budget control system?

                                                 Check

  - advertising budget summary
  - forward commitment summary
  - monthly list of expenditures
  - invoice approval system
  - supplier estimate system
■ Which suppliers do you use:
  - by type?
  - by size?
■ How do they compare on price with the market?
        Supplier   *Estimate*

■ On media, what is the achievement?
  - rate card versus actual
  - audience versus estimate
■ What timetable system is there?

9

Evaluating the Effect

TRYING TO FIND OUT

Advertising can take up a lot of time, and effort, and money. It is an expensive and serious process. Behind the campaign lies the need to justify it before it begins and to justify it after it has appeared.

It is not sufficient just to *do* advertising. For a professional and effective result, it is necessary also to *evaluate* it. Did it work? And how did it work? How far did it work? Were its objectives fulfilled? To what extent? And now what remains to be done?

As much as is possible, the advertiser has to find out. It is part of the responsibility of the campaign. Therefore, alongside the creative and media process there is often an accompanying strand of evaluations and research. Increasingly, the advertiser looks for *proof*, or evidence.

WHAT TO FIND OUT

The advertiser or the agency has to do two things:

1. carry out a plan of action
2. discover what happened.

There is a range of pressing reasons why the advertiser must find out. Among these are:

■ *The need to assess how far the objectives have been reached.* There was a main point in carrying out the campaign. Did the advertiser achieve this?

■ *The need to justify to management.* The advertising manager has to make a case in advance to the corporate management, to authorise the investment of funds. For self-protection or for professional clarity, the advertiser would be wise to show to management how well that money has been spent and what it has accomplished. It is an act of accountability.

■ *To learn for next time.* It is a learning process. Advertising campaigns progress, evolve and can always be improved. What went right this time? What could have worked better? What needs to be done for next time round?

Advertising agencies, in particular, are under some pressure to perform well and to show how well they have performed. Evaluation is a kind of self-protection as well as being another act of professional accountability.

It is, of course, crucial to determine what to evaluate. Here there are grounds for disagreement and for considerable misunderstanding. If the wrong thing is evaluated, or if the evaluation does not quite cover the relevant issues, then unreliable conclusions will be drawn. Many campaigns are subject to research that is extensive, expensive, ingenious – and faulty. So, wisdom lies in determining precisely what most needs to be learned. Light will need to be thrown on to a number of issues.

Campaign objectives

How far were these met? If they were to build up awareness, what is the awareness now? If they were to promote recall of the product specification, how far do people now recall it? If they were to obtain a favourable rating against competition, what is the perception of the product now against competition and how well does the product rate against those competitors?

Creative effectiveness

Just how well did the creative vehicle work? Did the audience like it, remember it, respond to it? What was the central theme of the creative approach and did it shift audience reactions to the product? Was the creative offer understood and accepted?

Effect on the audience

What did the audience think before and what do they think now? Have their attitudes changed? What do they know and feel about the product that they did not know before?

Problem solving

If the campaign set out to overcome a problem, how well did it do so? What was the problem before and how far does it now exist? What elements of the problem still remain to be dealt with?

What needs to be found out has to be defined as thoroughly and as fully as any other part of the advertising equation. If the question is unclear, there cannot possibly be a complete answer.

WHAT SOURCES ARE THERE FOR INFORMATION?

Defining the questions to be asked may be easier than obtaining answers. In practice, the advertiser only has a limited number of ways in which to obtain the information.

Research

Research studies may be commissioned. There is a very wide range of research techniques available for checking on advertising. Indeed, advertisement research is a kind of sub-industry in itself. A large number of campaigns are researched, some before they appear, some while the campaign is operating and some examine the campaign after it has concluded to assess the overall effect.

Research is possible and relevant, but only when the scale of the campaign justifies it and when there are sufficient funds available. Advertising research can be highly expensive, and a great many advertisers do not have the resources to pay for it.

Examination of sales data

The physical effects may be assessed; that is, how far sales have been influenced. Sales figures may be examined, for traces of sales movement or sales trends in relation to advertising activities. But here again, there are limits. Not all advertisers have sales data. Many are in fields where sales data are not obtainable or are not relevant. Others may have only limited access to sales information.

It would also be helpful to correlate advertising activity to market share. How does the advertising affect share of market over time? This would be evidence of great importance, but here again many advertisers do not have share of market information readily available and some, indeed, are not in situations where share of market is a relevant concept. Local authority advertising is just one example.

Information from intermediaries

Where the production process sells through intermediaries, then these may be a helpful source of information. A very large number of advertisers do use sales intermediaries – dealers and distributors, wholesalers and retailers, brokers and agents – from manufacturers of physical goods, to the travel and holiday trade, to insurance and financial services. The intermediary may be asked for a view of the effect of any recent advertising, or to provide evidence of sales movement.

Here too there are limits. Many advertisers do not use intermediaries, and even if they do the intermediaries may not have precise enough information, or may not be in a position to supply information, or may perhaps be biased, or too busy to respond.

Information from branches

While an organisation may not use a system of intermediaries, it may have its own branch network. This is particularly so in the retail field, or banking, or catering or entertainment. In some cases, an advertiser may have a network of franchisees or local representatives. These also may be called on to provide an assessment of any local advertising effects or data on customer reactions.

Direct response

In the field of direct response advertising, it is easier to perceive the relation between advertising output and customer output. Sales returns, or at least response data, are themselves a kind of monitor of advertising effect.

Even where the organisation may not ultimately sell through direct response or mail order, the advertising may have some kind of response ingredient: a coupon, a telephone number, an enquiry address. The level of contacts through these can at least be calculated, to see what response levels there have been in proportion to advertising effort.

The sales force
Where an organisation employs a sales force, it too may be used to help draw up a picture of what the advertising has done. Although there are limitations as to what the sales force can provide, used sensibly and diplomatically it can be a source of considerable insight.

Let us look at some of these methods more closely.

TO RESEARCH OR NOT TO RESEARCH

The first main tool of information is advertising research. How usable is it? There are a number of conditions to observe.

Is there an absolute need for research?

Since research costs large amounts of money, is it imperative that information is obtained? It is sometimes nice to know, but not vital. It may in many cases be a luxury, not an essential. But in many cases it is indispensable.

Is there a problem area?

On the whole, research checks out problems or looks at areas of difficulty. Certain types of advertising do not work against a problem but against an immediate need. Sales announcements for retailers, announcements of new interest rates for banks, urgent recruitment advertisements, advertising to distributors have basically to state a message, short, sharp and to the point.

Where there is no problem, research may provide reassurance. But only in those circumstances where reassurance is a valid idea itself.

Is there enough money?

Many advertisers may wish for research, but just do not have the funds for it. This is a considerable difficulty. There is a danger that advertising research may become a tool for the larger advertiser. There are ways of reducing cost, or achieving an economic price, but the smaller advertiser finds increasing strain in funding research.

Is the expenditure in proportion to the campaign?

Smaller campaigns may not be able to justify research. A £10,000 advertising expenditure would find it hard to justify a £10,000 research budget. There has to be a sense of balance. Indeed, it is probably the case that most smaller campaigns do not use advertising research.

Can the research be used?

While research provides reassurance, it is there to throw up evidence of areas where action needs to be taken. If the research cannot be used, if no action can be taken on it, then the point of doing it is reduced.

Is there time?

Many advertising programmes happen fast. If the advertising is to appear rapidly, there may be too little time to carry out a proper research study, let alone put it to use.

So, the rules for the employment of research are a matter of commonsense:

■ use research when there is a clear need
■ use research when you can take action on the results
■ use research when there is enough time
■ use research when you have sufficient funds to obtain a proper research programme. Do not buy in second-rate research to save money
■ use research when the expenditure is in proportion to the size of the overall advertising programme or the importance of the campaign.

WHAT RESEARCH?

Advertising research covers a wide span of types. The strategy here is to fit the research type to the problem posed. Research is carried out on a need-to-know basis. So, what do we need to know? And therefore what research method will provide this best? Characteristic areas of doubt include the following:

■ *The creative strategy:* does it match customer requirements?
■ *The creative concept:* does the audience accept it and find it valid?
■ *The creative communication or vehicle:* does the audience understand it?
■ *Awareness:* does the campaign enhance audience awareness?
■ *Recall:* is there clear recall of the product name, or specification, or indeed of the advertising itself?
■ *Campaign effect:* what does the campaign achieve overall?
■ *Positives and negatives:* are there any negatives that can now be eliminated, or positives that can be enhanced?

There are two main ways to categorise research methods:

1. by time
2. by type.

Research by time

There are three points at which research may be helpful:

1. *Before the advertising begins:* pre-testing, to remove problems in advance.
2. *Just after the advertising begins:* to evaluate recall, in light of real experience.
3. *When the advertising has ended:* to measure the cumulative effect.

The budget may be large enough to cover all three stages. For the largest of advertisers this may be so. A £20 million budget can accommodate a £70,000 research spend. But for the average advertiser, the choice must be made: when is it tactically most useful to research? One piece of research only is most likely for many advertisers.

Research by type

As is famously known, research is divided into two major categories:

1. quantitative
2. qualitative

The former deals in numbers, in scale, in percentages. Typically using a large sample to produce simple replies to a standard questionnaire, which are then percentaged out. The latter probes smaller groups, in a less structured, more open way, and produces hypotheses or general impressions.

Much advertising research has swung to the latter, but there are now signs of a swing back. If absolute numbers are imperative, then quantitative research is needed; if impressions or insights are valuable then qualitative research may be preferred.

Deciding then on which route to take – testing pre- or post-advertising, and quantitative or qualitative methods – means that specific research programmes can be formulated. There are a number of more commonly used types:

■ *Usage and attitude studies:* how the product is used, and how it is perceived. This will help in the formulation of strategies.
■ *Market or competitive mapping:* where the product or service fits in the market, against competitors or against customer use. This too will help in the formulation of strategies.
■ *Awareness studies:* what are awareness levels? Against competition? This again will aid the production of an advertising strategy.
■ *Concept tests:* how does a proposed creative concept rate? This is vital to know, to assess the relevance of a proposition or promise.
■ *Communications test:* how well does a particular piece of advertising communicate? Is it understood? Can it be read clearly? Or seen or heard clearly? Does the audience get the message? Here advertisements can be shown in a workshop, or rough or unfinished form.
■ *Recall tests:* having seen the advertising, do the audience remember it? What features can they recall? Do they recall the product name, or product plus?
■ *Campaign penetration studies:* what overall effect has the campaign had? Not just one advertisement, not perhaps just the advertising, but the whole of the communications campaign. That is, the effect on customer perceptions, or awareness, or usage or attitudes.
■ *Pre- and post-comparison:* how has the advertising affected people, in comparison with the situation before the advertising appeared? What trends or movements appear? This will probably involve doing two stages of research – before and after.

■ *Tracking studies:* these work over time, and may involve an ongoing series of research programmes. How does the product or service stand in the market, over time, in relation to its competitors? How is it perceived, what are its values, what are its strengths and weakness?

Of this array of types, it should be said that probably the best used or most flexibly used of techniques is currently that of group discussions, quickly put together and fluidly conducted, which will throw light on concepts or on pieces of communication, two of the key areas of information vital for both agency and client.

WHO DOES THE RESEARCH?

The advertiser may not be a research specialist, and this is an area where expertise is essential. So there is considerable use of specialist research agencies or research consultants – unless the advertiser is large enough to afford an in-house research department. When this is not the case, the advertiser has two means:

1. Use the advertising agency: where the agency has its own research service, or can commission an outside research supplier.
2. Use an independent service: the client directly commissions the research consultant. This tends in practice to be the more common way. An independent service is considered more objective, with less of a vested interest, although the advertising agency should be kept fully informed.

Where the advertiser does not have the required research contacts, help can be obtained from the research trade body – the Market Research Society.

USING SALES DATA

Where market research is unaffordable or unobtainable, the advertiser may turn to sales information for guidance. Clearly there are limitations. Advertising is not the only force that affects sales. The purpose of the advertising may not necessarily be a sales one. Or it may work too long term to show up comfortably in short-term sales analyses.

But bearing these reservations carefully in mind, it is nevertheless practical for the advertiser to see what the sales data may have to say. And to begin, the advertiser must ensure that there is a satisfactory provision of such data. The communications department must insist that it, too, receives the information, in a form that will be helpful. It will want to know. Information needed includes:

■ what current sales are. Sales data up to date
■ what sales were before the advertising and after the advertising
■ what sales were in the same time last year
■ sales data will also be helpful by distributor type
■ any way of establishing market share data would be helpful, where market share is a relevant concept
■ sales data by region are also desirable, especially where there may be regional differences in the creative or media approach.

As a result of these needs, it is prudent to build into an advertising plan a structure for sales data before the advertising begins. It is up to the advertising manager to initiate this and negotiate it with the sales force.

DIRECT RESPONSE INFORMATION

If it is at all possible, the communications department should try to establish the level and volume of direct responses from the advertising. This means setting up a suitable system to record such responses:

■ number of telephone calls
■ number of postal enquiries
■ number of overall enquiries
■ number of brochures sent out.

Two things are necessary here:

1. A means of sourcing the enquiry. The simple way is to key advertisement coupons, and to ask telephone enquiries: where did you hear about us, please?
2. A method of recording each such enquiry.

Having done this, it then becomes possible to analyse the information and break down advertising response into component elements, such as:

■ enquiries per publication or per insertion
■ enquiries for different offers or advertisement headlines.

It is more helpful still to go beyond this, if at all possible, and to correlate the two factors discussed so far, sales data and response data. This will produce a picture of response on something on the following lines:

■ number of enquiries (say, per publication)
■ cost per enquiry
■ number of sales conversions
■ cost per sales conversion
■ average value per sales conversion.

A view soon emerges of the comparative effectiveness of certain types of media or of creative appeal.

INTERMEDIARIES AND BRANCHES

While the use of the intermediaries as a source of information may be hard to accomplish, it is worth attempting. The intermediary is face to face with the customer, as is the company branch. Some helpful playback on advertising effect may be possible, and could be very instructive.

The advertiser does not wish to relinquish control, nor can they impose a workload upon organisations which are nominally independent. But feedback from the marketplace is a reasonable thing to want, and the intermediary or company branch may willingly cooperate, if approached carefully. There are various means to achieve this:

■ *A distributor or branch panel:* some advertisers form regular panels of intermediaries, to comment on advertising plans, or to report reactions from the field. One method used is to send out questionnaires, by post. An example of this can be seen in Figure 9.1. These responses can be tabulated, and percentaged out if this is helpful.

SPRING ADVERTISING PROGRAMME
Assessment (ring the result you experienced)

▓ Customer enquiries during campaign → much higher-higher-same-lower-
very low

▓ Customer awareness of campaign → very high-quite high-indifferent-low-
very low

▓ Customer requests for literature → much above average-above average-
average-below average-much below
average

▓ Average size of customer orders → much higher-higher-same-lower-much lower

Figure 9.1   *Spring advertising programme*

▓ *Telephone questionnaires:* it may be possible to draw up a list of cooperative dealers, and get them to agree to providing rapid-response information. When questions arise, they are telephoned and will be answered informally and swiftly.

KEEP IT IN THE BANK

Evaluation needs to be filed, stored away for use another day. Many advertisers find difficulty in retaining their records of performance but these will be invaluable for reference and comparison in the future. It is vital to maintain a bank of information on past events, if possible in a standard form so that evaluations can be built up over time. A typical format might be that shown in Figure 9.2. A copy of the schedule would be attached for any campaign.

MEDIA EVALUATION

This is part of the media planning exercise. It is invaluable, too, for maintaining a record of media achievement during a campaign. How does the schedule perform? What was attained? Information needed might be:

▓ combined circulations

ADVERTISING PERFORMANCE ANALYSIS

Product _____   Date/period of advertising _____

Media used _____   Budget_____

Sales volume _____

Market share _____

Consumer awareness score _____

Consumer attitude summary _____

Distributor attitude summary_____

Figure 9.2   *Advertising performance analysis*

▓ total coverage
▓ average frequency, or opportunities to see
▓ average cost per '000 over the schedule
▓ cost per '000 by media type
▓ audience composition
▓ rate card total cost versus actual total cost.

The advertising agency or media independent will be asked to supply this. Where none is employed, certain chosen media will be asked to produce their own schedule analysis – and may do so out of friendship. A combination of circulation figures (such as the ABC), together with data from the larger media surveys (such as the National Readership Survey) will suffice for the bulk of what is required.

EVALUATING CREATIVE PERFORMANCE

The creative content of advertisements can be looked at in the light of different methods of evaluation:

▓ research approaches
▓ panels of distributors
▓ scrutiny of sales data.

But there is still a large element of judgement. Research cannot cover all eventualities.

The judgement of the individual advertiser will always come into play. There is nothing to be ashamed of in this. The advertiser will see evaluation by personal judgement as being a professional act in its own right, sharpened by professional experience.

Where possible, creative evaluation is helped by having alternatives, or a range of options to compare. It is so much easier to select or analyse among a number of possibilities, rather than comment on just one.

EVALUATION CHECKLIST

- What are the problems you need to solve?
- What is the advertising setting out to do?
- How does the advertising seem to accomplish this:
  Specify and check out
  - by strategy?
  - by concept?
  - by offer or promise?
  - by tone of voice or advertising style?
- What is the basic form of communication in the advertising?
- How well does this work?
  Specify and check out
  - understandability of main proposition
  - understandability of subsidiary arguments
  - recall of main claim
  - readability of headline
  - readability of body-copy
  - visibility of TV film
  - clarity of storyline
  - readability of soundtrack
  - visibility of logotype
- What level of awareness has been achieved?
- What level of playback is there?
- How do customer/consumer attitudes now stand?
- What do distributors feel?
- What does the sales force feel?
- Who will carry out evaluation?
- When?
- By what method?
- Cost of evaluation

10

Recruitment Advertising

THE GENERAL NEED

A separate chapter is devoted to recruitment advertising because it is for many organisations one of the most used forms of advertising. Indeed, many people find that recruitment advertising is the first thing they do. Many smaller organisations which do not customarily regard themselves as carrying out any advertising whatsoever do indeed run recruitment advertisements at one time or the other.

The need for staff is considerable. As part of the process of finding staff it may be helpful to place an advertisement. While this is not a commercial function with a commercial process, nevertheless recruitment advertising does follow the principles of advertising in general. Because of its widespread use it is important to devote space to it.

Overall, recruitment advertising is a major factor in the advertising world as a whole. It represents a turnover of many millions of pounds, is the source of very considerable income for the media, newspapers in particular, and sustains a large number of specialist advertising agencies. So, recruitment advertising is both a much used category within advertising overall and a kind of sub-industry in itself.

WHO CARRIES IT OUT?

For most communications activities, the activities required are usually centred on the communications department or advertising manager. But recruitment advertising is an exception. In a large number of organisations, recruitment advertising is carried out by the personnel or human resources department. There are, indeed, three ways in which recruitment advertising can be conducted by those who need it:

1. in small organisations, by the general manager (who may carry out all the other communications activities too)
2. by the personnel/human resources department
3. by the advertising department.

The value of the latter route is that it enables all the company's advertising activities to be coordinated and integrated under one authority. It saves time for the personnel people. It enables the media buying operation to be totally coordinated, and the organisation's presentation of itself to the outside world to have consistency and coherence. So, many organisations will use the advertising department – where it exists. They in turn will instruct the advertising agency as part of the agency's normal function.

Conversely, it may overload the advertising department, deflect it from its main purpose, and make things overcomplicated and protracted for the personnel department. Nor is recruitment an expertise which the advertising manager will necessarily have.

For this reason, many organisations prefer to keep recruitment advertising within the personnel department. They can plan it as part of their wider strategy for attracting staff applications and do so directly without any intermediaries. Many personnel departments retain their own advertising agency. Indeed, it is common for organisations to retain two different advertising agencies. One for commercial, corporate or marketing purposes, reporting to the communications manager, and one solely for recruitment activities, reporting to the personnel or human resources manager.

The choice and method are often a matter of size, volume of recruitment assignments, workloads and the amount of time and people the personnel department has available. It may also be a matter of location. If, for example, the communications department is situated at head office but the main personnel department is situated at the factory site, it may simply be more convenient to conduct the recruitment advertising locally.

WHEN TO ADVERTISE

Not all recruitment needs are met by advertising. Organisations have a wide portfolio of means of recruiting staff, and need to control carefully the amount of advertisements used, in the interests of efficiency and economy.

The personnel function is faced with requests for staff from various operating divisions of the organisation. It has to find the staff. Or at least find applicants for jobs, even if the operating divisions are allowed to make the final selection. There are in practice two situations:

1. where the personnel function attracts applicants and makes the selection
2. where the personnel function attracts applicants and the managers of the operating divisions make the selection.

Certainly in the case of senior posts, the latter way is more common. But whatever procedure is adopted, the personnel manager is faced with a request to find staff. In which case, a strategy for this recruitment assignment needs to be developed. That is, how best to attract applications for this particular job vacancy?

The best means must be adopted. These can include the following.

■ *Use of an employment agency.* These exist to identify, interview and shortlist candidates for jobs. They often specialise, eg employment agencies for secretaries, for engineers, for contract staff. They may also specialise by industry, eg employment agencies for the catering trade, or for the petroleum and petrochemical industry, or for the various sectors of the computer industry and high-technology. But they do cost money. Usually a substantial proportion of the first year's salary.
■ *Executive search companies.* These help recruit more senior grades of staff. Selection of a key executive is often regarded as a major step, sometimes a crucial step for the future of the company. It is therefore commonly entrusted to specialists with the experience and expertise to find suitable recruits. There may be very few potential candidates available, and finding them may be difficult and time consuming, so outside help may be essential. But this again is an expensive method.

■ *Job Centres and public authorities.* Organisations may turn to the facilities made available to the community by government operations, eg Job Centres. These services are usually free and are suitable as a first port of call for various grades of staff – but usually less senior.

■ *Direct recruitment.* Organisations may recruit directly, by going straight to applicants. This often takes the form of visits to recruitment locations. For example:
  - the 'milk round' visits to universities to select graduate trainees
  - visits to schools and colleges, for junior entrants
  - participation in local 'job fairs', where recruiter and recruited may meet face to face
  - scrutiny of registers, direct approach to individuals
  - use of existing bank of CVs, from previous job searches

■ *Databases.* Use can also be made of the growing network of personnel databases – lists kept on computer of possible suitable staff:
  - either those assembled from past job applicants
  - or, those employed within an industry or in other firms.

But this, too, can be expensive. Or regarded as an unacceptable concept. In which case, a need for advertising may also arise.

There are two situations when recruitment advertising is employed:

1. by itself, when nothing else is done, or needed
2. as part of a larger package of recruitment activities.

There are many occasions when a recruitment advertisement is run by itself, as the sole activity, and when nothing else is necessary. Such reasons for concentrating on recruitment advertising are varied.

Firstly, it is fast. If a vacancy arises on a Thursday, a suitable advertisement could run that Sunday. If there is no time to spare, an advertisement can bring the quickest response. Run an advertisement and you can fill the vacancy in a week.

Recruitment advertising can save money. Often it is the cheapest thing to do. A local press advertisement can cost £50, and bring in two recruits. Use an employment agency, and they will charge 15 per cent of the first year's salary (or more) which could cost say £5,500 for an average-level salary for average-level jobs. Search and selection consultants would charge a lot more than this for senior staff.

Often the use of an employment agency is just not financially possible. Or does not make financial sense.

Of course, an advertisement for staff does mean that the organisation must now do what the employment agency would otherwise do: it must receive and handle the applications, process them and conduct interviews.

A hundred applicants, telephoning and writing. A hundred sets of records and application forms, perhaps 10 or 15 first interviews, then a series of final interviews may all take time and cost money. In the end, the company must (or should, even if it does not) carry out a calculation. Which is the cheaper – a recruitment advertisement or use of an employment agency? The calculation goes:

■ advertising:
  – cost of advertisement £A
  – cost of handling, processing and interview time £B
  – total £C
■ employment agency:
  – cost of employment agency service and fee £D.

In very many cases, advertising will prove the cheaper, even with all costs factored in. There are also other factors:

■ *It may be mandatory.* In some areas, such as public authorities or public corporations, it is part of a given personnel procedure that all staff vacancies must be advertised. This is common.
■ *It is convenient.* There is no need to bring in outside people. The process is simple, fast, direct and uncluttered.
■ *It can do a corporate image job.* A value of recruitment advertising is that it, too, says something about the organisation. It is a message not only to potential staff but to the outside world in general. A recruitment advertisement may say: we are expanding, we are attracting more staff, we are building more facilities, we are being a success, we are important. Take note of us. It is an opportunity to project the company. In many cases, it is as important an opportunity as any other.

For this mix of reasons, recruitment advertising is prevalent. The organisation will do two things. It will search its files and see if it has any applicants readily on hand. If not, it may then draw up a recruitment strategy in which advertising is central. To save time, to save money, to save complications.

WHEN NOT TO ADVERTISE

The organisation needs to consider the implications of recruitment advertising very carefully. There are occasions when it would not be prudent, and – as in all other communications activities – it needs to be analysed with rigour.

Cost

At times, advertising may be more costly than other means. If a senior executive is sought, and a large space is required in *The Sunday Times* and *The Daily Telegraph*, the media cost may actually be as much as the fee of an executive search company.

Cost comparisons must always be made.

Sensitivity

Some recruitment assignments are highly confidential. It is not therefore advisable to advertise them.

Internal resources

The organisation may not have the people, the time or the facilities to devote to the interviewing and selection task. Endless telephone calls, large quantities of application forms, series of lengthy interviews can be a terrible bother and completely disruptive. For the smaller organisation in particular, it may just be far simpler to transfer the whole burden on to an employment consultancy.

Specialist expertise

Recruitment is itself a skill, which the employer may not necessarily possess. Or the job on offer may be of a very specialised kind, calling for a specialised recruiter. Again, an outside service may be preferable. To advertise or not to advertise is therefore a matter of weighing up the conflicting advantages and disadvantages, at all times.

THE SCALE OF ACTIVITY

The recruitment advertising will vary according to the nature of the position offered. But it typically can operate on one of three scales.

The local

For junior staff, for factory personnel, for part-time or contract staff, for casual vacancies, it should be sufficient just to advertise purely locally. Many organisations consist of a set of local establishments, and advertising usually clusters round them, from site to site. Often there is no need at all to go wider.

The national

For more senior staff, or for highly specialist staff, it may be necessary or unavoidable to go national. Either by using national media covering that level of appointment (eg national press) or national media covering that category of skill or expertise (eg national professional or technical magazines).

The international

For very senior appointments, or for exceptionally specialist posts, it may be necessary to go international, to try to recruit from other countries. This is rarer, but growing in use.

SELECTING RECRUITMENT MEDIA

Many media have a recruitment competence. Many indeed set out to attract recruitment revenue, and therefore build up their facilities for this.

Selecting recruitment media follows the same system or process as other types of advertising media selection, namely:

■ who is the target market?
■ what is the budget, or how much is the organisation prepared to spend on recruiting staff?

Targeting

This is defined by two things:

1. The grade or level of staff required. A job description is needed, which will specify precisely, with as much accuracy as possible, the exact grade or employment type.
2. The scale. Whether this needs to be a local search or a national search.

The budget

Some organisations prefer to keep a job-by-job financial basis for recruitment. Each search will carry its own advertising budget, depending on the value and salary cost of the jobs involved. Others may prefer to operate a total annual budget, so that they know what they will allocate overall to recruitment – as part of the wider corporate budgeting.

Having defined the type of appointment, and the budget available, candidate media will then be considered.

Preference is usually given to those with appointments sections, or situations vacant columns. People may purchase these media primarily to look for jobs. The employer and the applicant will come together There will be high page traffic and readership, strong noting and attention to recruitment advertising. Specialist recruitment sections maximise the power of recruitment advertising, reduce wastage and provide value for money.

Local press

This is heavily read for local jobs and usually operates substantial recruitment sections. It is most suitable for lower level jobs, jobs of a purely local nature, part-time jobs, local government jobs.

Local authorities are among the largest recruitment advertisers in Britain. Many traditionally have spent in excess of a million pounds a year. The local press is their primary outlet.

It has the merit of being comparatively cheap.

National newspapers

Much of the national press runs substantial recruitment sections or jobs columns. This is a prime source of income for them. The most used national newspapers are those:

■ providing high coverage of more senior job levels
■ providing high coverage of specialist areas.

The Daily Telegraph famously has strong coverage of middle-manager grades. *The Sunday Times* has a strong coverage of executive levels, while *The Guardian* has a strong coverage of media and publishing areas. The *Financial Times* covers financial posts.

Professional and technical magazines

These often cover key industries or occupation groups, and will provide concentrated readership against a particular grade of job vacancy. They are often bought just for job hunting purposes, and will run extensive situations vacant sections. Using them will save time, money and wastage.

Where a profession or occupation may have a range of magazines covering it, there is commonly one leader or title with the greatest recruitment pull. This is, by definition, the first choice for advertising. For example, *New Civil Engineer* has a wide and respected position in civil engineering; *Campaign* magazine is the most read for advertising industry jobs; *The Times Educational Supplement* is a power in teacher recruitment.

The bulk of recruitment advertising uses newspapers or magazines. Many campaigns stop there and use nothing else. But other media can have useful recruitment applications, if considered carefully.

Posters

These can be used for large-scale recruitment jobs. They can be used in stations or transportation sites or near a factory site, to attract passers-by. Such posters are more suitable for lower job grades.

Radio

This may be used effectively on a local level. Radio can impart urgency, make a job sound attractive and reach a reasonable local audience. Radio is often used in conjunction with local press, and is again more suitable for recruiting larger numbers of people. It is cheap and rapid.

TV

This has a much lower usage, for reasons of cost and selectivity. Smaller TV stations may be affordable, for local vacancies, but metropolitan TV stations have not so far been attractive. With the growth of TV facilities this might change.

Cinema

This could cover a limited area, but is little used.

Direct mail

Targeting potential staff by the use of databases is increasing, and may increase still further. It has the merit of reaching people of interest. On the other hand, mailings are expensive pro rata, are unsolicited, and may be rejected. They can be very wasteful.

Mailing has more potential against selective, higher job grade assignments than against large number projects.

Exhibitions

Job fairs, travelling circuses, recruitment roadshows, visits to universities and schools and so on are on the increase. However they take time and money, and are usually more usable by larger organisations, or those that recruit in large numbers, such as the police, nursing service, army and so on.

Telephone

Where potential candidates can be identified and isolated, telephone contact may also be used. This is, indeed, a primary form of contact employed by 'head-hunters' or executive search consultancies. Again, it is more practical for small-scale assignments, or for higher level appointments.

Internet

Although limited in coverage, Internet possesses the potential for considerable pulling-power in reaching job candidates, especially internationally. And, importantly, it is interactive. Candidates can e-mail back their CVs.

THE MEDIA PLAN

On the whole, media plans for recruitment advertising are simple and uncomplicated, as follows:

1. Select the most appropriate medium or media for the vacancy.
2. Limit the selection. Often one advertisement will do in one publication, if sufficient coverage is obtainable.
3. Limit the combination. It may be necessary to combine two media to be certain of coverage; eg *The Daily Telegraph* and *The Sunday Times* or *New Civil Engineer* and *The Daily Telegraph*. It is unusual to have a long schedule list because key major media will be sufficient to do the job.
4. Use reinforcement media if the budget justifies. If the assignment is a large-scale one, say to recruit 20 staff for a new factory in Leeds, then a mix of media may be used; eg (Leeds) *Yorkshire Evening Post*, local radio, poster outside factory site. Where the recruitment job is more limited, it will be too expensive and wasteful.
5. Control the size of space. There are two basic press positions:
   - classified lineage
   - classified display.
   Much recruitment advertising is carried out on a lineage or classified basis, appearing in classified columns and newspaper set. This may be all that is needed. But larger, display space may be required either to carry a longer message or to gain greater impact. In which case the rule is that the size of display space is in proportion to the value of the job. Also, size may be needed to offset the clutter of general recruitment pages. But there is an optimum size. Full pages in magazines are rarely used or needed.
6. Control the frequency: one insertion may be all that is required. Read the results of that insertion, and have a follow-up insertion only when it is clear that it is necessary to do so.

THE ELEMENTS OF THE MESSAGE

Here again, recruitment advertising can be simple and uncomplicated, but needs to be as persuasive as any other kind of advertising.

Strong headline
The advertisement needs to identify immediately the job being offered, and the grade of employee to be considered.

Job description
The copy must clearly state what the job is, what the applicant does, and how the job functions.

Salary
In most cases, this is a central feature, and must be boldly stated. In some cases, as with senior staff or sensitive positions, salaries will not be stated and will be open to negotiation or discussion.

Location
The site of the job must be clearly presented.

The organisation
It is usual to include a statement about the organisation, for reassurance sake, or to help the respondent decide.

Action needed
A clear statement of next action, who to contact and how it is required, with a detailed name, address and (sometimes) telephone number, fax number or e-mail number.

Corporate element
If possible, the advertisement should adhere to corporate styling, general design approaches, use of the corporate logotype etc.

Benefits
Above all, the advertisement must specify, identify and promote the benefit of the job. Advertisements do not just sell jobs, they sell the value of the job to the applicant – what the job can do for them personally.

USING AN AGENCY

The advertiser has a choice of four routes, for the implementation of a programme. In practice a mix may often be used:

1. doing it in house

2. asking the media for help and advice
3. using the general advertising agency
4. using a specialist recruitment agency.

Where the workload is low, the in-house way may suffice. Or, specialist media may be called in and the recruitment department will help, if possible. Where the workload is higher, or where specialist creative work is needed, then the general advertising agency may be called in. When the workload is intense, a specialist recruitment agency may be desirable, and that is the method employed by many organisations.

The specialist agency may be preferable:

■ when there is a constant flow of work and a large expenditure
■ when specialist creative and planning skills are required
■ when extra services are required.

Recruitment advertising agencies provide a range of services:

■ specialist planning experience
■ specialist copywriting services, often specialised industry by industry
■ in-depth knowledge of the media
■ postbox facilities, handling replies to advertisements
■ CV handling: taking in and processing CVs
■ sifting and screening: the agency might prepare a shortlist
■ interviewing and consultancy, where it has a licence to do so.

Once again, the determining element in selecting a resource is cost.

RECRUITMENT CHECKLIST

■ Who has to be recruited:
  - by number?
  - by job grade?
  - by location?
■ What is the job specification? And salary?
■ When must the vacancy be filled and the new job begin?
■ Who in the organisation must interview and decide?
■ How much time do these people have?
■ How competitive is the job market for this vacancy?
■ Who are the competitors, and how does this job compare?
■ Is there any degree of confidentiality?
■ How many people seem to be available at this time?
■ What is the recruitment advertising budget?
■ Are there any corporate do's and don'ts about the advertising?
■ What are the available media?

Category	Medium	Size	Cost

■ What are the copy dates?
■ Which media deliver:
  - greatest coverage of candidates?
  - greatest economy?
  - closest readership and attention?
  - greatest authority?
■ Who will handle CVs and applications?
■ Who will originate and produce the advertisement?
■ Check for:
  - strength of design
  - impact of headline
  - accuracy of job description
  - clarity of overall benefit offered
  - persuasiveness
  - corporate design elements.

11

Selecting Suppliers and Agencies

THE SUPPLIERS NEEDED

Advertising is a collaborative process. The advertiser requires a variety of jobs to be done, and a large number of these jobs have to be subcontracted. They have to be done in whole or in part by outside suppliers. An advertising campaign is indeed, in this sense, a compound of items bought in from suppliers, with the advertiser himself acting as a kind of coordinator or commander-in-chief. It is therefore essential that the advertiser organises this network of suppliers in an effective way, for three overriding reasons:

1. *Quality:* the advertiser has to achieve the maximum quality from these varying suppliers, or else the campaign will be mediocre.
2. *Timing:* if the suppliers do not act promptly, or keep to the promised delivery dates, then the timing of the advertising programme may go to pieces, with disastrous consequences.
3. *Cost:* the suppliers can keep to budgets, supply value, maintain reasonable prices or go out of control and ruin the advertising expenditure. Moderate cost and high value are requisites of any campaign.

The advertiser produces a large volume of publicity elements and is therefore involved with a large circle of suppliers. Much of the advertiser's time is taken up with instructing, dealing with, checking and communicating with suppliers. Many of these, however, regard themselves as professionals or industries in their own right and do not look on themselves as 'suppliers'.

But suppliers they essentially are, and they have to be evaluated in the same sense as all suppliers to commerce are classically evaluated – in terms of quality, timing and price. Such suppliers may include the following:

- *Advertising agencies:* a large number of advertisers use agencies, though by no means all.
- *Media independents:* professionals in buying and selling media space.
- *Studios or creative groups:* who may supply finished artwork, graphics or creative ideas of any kind.
- *Photographers:* who produce a variety of photographic work, some general, some highly specialised.
- *Photographic libraries:* supplying stock photographs, as an alternative to procuring new photography.
- *Design group:* as against the general finished artwork studio, the advertiser may use a specialist design activity for a specialist design purpose, ie specialist designers for packaging or for corporate image – logotype and name styles, letterheads, stationery, exterior presentation of the organisation in a multitude of ways.
- *Typesetters:* producers of typesetting for required print items.
- *Retouchers:* retouching and improving colour transparencies.
- *Colour houses:* who may process colour work, produce colour separations and deliver colour film.
- *Printers:* different types of printer for different types of work. Literature production breaks down into categories of print for which certain specialisms are more suitable.
- *Public relations:* there is an overlap between PR and advertising, and an advertiser may retain a public relations consultant to do a range of jobs, among which may be some activities bordering on general advertising areas or at least publicity areas, such as exhibitions or mailing, otherwise performed through an advertising agency.
- *Direct mail house:* the use of direct mail is now a central function. The advertiser may use one direct mail supplier for an all-through job, or specialist suppliers for specialist aspects, such as:

- list suppliers or database providers
- design and production of mailshots
- fulfilment, the physical process of mailing.

▓ *Exhibition work:* here again, the advertiser may use an all-through exhibition consultant, or several suppliers for specialist parts of the process and in particular:
- exhibition stand designers
- stand fitters, constructors and builders.

▓ *Film production:* the advertiser will subcontract to production companies who will deliver the production, direction and shooting of any films required, and who will also cover specialist aspects such as:
- set and costume design and production
- location search
- specialist casting.

▓ *Music:* if needed for a film, music may be commissioned via a film production company. But if the advertiser requires music for other purposes this may be obtained (via musicians' agents) direct from music writers, who can also arrange recording sessions.

▓ *Audio-visuals:* there is an enormous use today of audio-visuals (AVs). While film production companies can be used, many advertisers call on a network of specialist AV houses, who have substantial experience in a variety of audio-visual fields, corporate, training, presentations to customers, sales conferences etc. The finished material often takes the form of videos or CD-ROM.

▓ *Market research:* the substantial level of advertisement testing and communication research has led to the development of a wide network of research suppliers, again many highly specialist.

▓ *Telemarketing:* the enormous growth of telemarketing in the recent past has led to the growth of a wide number of telemarketing organisations, specialists in the construction and implementation of telemarketing programmes. Some may be general practitioners across the whole field of direct marketing and some operate for telemarketing alone.

▓ *Circulate distributors:* again, specialists in the physical distribution of leaflets and circulars, by door-to-door and other means.

▓ *Computers, computer graphics and multimedia:* an enormous expansion is taking place in the use of the computer for publicity purposes, in computer graphics, computerised demonstration or the technique of multimedia, which can combine various computerised applications in a flexible way. Here again, specialist suppliers are necessary.

■ An Internet Service Provider (ISP), for accessing the World Wide Web. There can be two services needed:
  - Web Site design
  - Internet access.

■ *Visual aids and presentation materials:* slide designers and producers and other suppliers of specialist presentation work also comprise a network of specialist expertise.

■ *Merchandise or industrial gift suppliers:* for buying-in the multitude of merchandise commonly required for business gifts or sales promotions, ranging from calendars to diaries to desk sets, to T-shirts and much else.

Faced with this panoply of specialists, buying-in advertising materials may seem endlessly daunting. Or, a stimulating challenge.

WHEN TO CONTRACT– AND SUBCONTRACT

The advertiser can deal with the matter of obtaining advertising services in one of three ways:

1. doing this internally, within the organisation
2. using an advertising agency for main purposes, but obtaining the remainder directly
3. contracting the bulk of requirements out to an advertising agency or other main supplier.

There are a number of key criteria to observe, when making this choice.

Size of organisation
If there are few people in the organisation, or the advertiser concerned is perhaps a sole proprietor, then one of two situations may arise.

1. There are too few people around, with too little time to handle the amount of work needed. It therefore has to be contracted out.
2. The scale of the work and the size of the advertiser are so small that there is no need to contract it out.

Larger organisations may, of course, have the staff with the time to spare to handle these requirements.

Size of funds

The advertiser may not be able to afford to bring in a consultancy. Or, the expenditure may be too low to make this a practical proposition.

One small recruitment advertisement in one local paper does not justify a fully-fledged recruitment agency, nor would it usually cover its costs.

Scale and extent of the workload

One-off, non-repeating *ad hoc* jobs may not need to be contracted out. A heavy and continuing workload, with a wide variety of tasks, may have to be.

Expertise

If the advertising task is of a highly specialised kind or calls for particular skills, the advertiser may necessarily have to contract this out to agencies with those skills.

Time

Sometimes delegation takes time that the advertiser does not have. Sometimes delegating saves the advertiser time that otherwise would be wasted.

Confidentiality

If the matter in hand is particularly sensitive, or the advertiser requires complete confidentiality with no possibility of a 'leak', then handling the work in-house may again be preferable.

Available services

There may be no services available locally of an appropriate kind, so the advertiser again may prefer to work in house.

But for reasons of time, money and convenience, a large proportion of advertisers do in practice use an outside consultant, agency or media independent service. To summarise:

■ *When to do it yourself*: the advertiser may handle the advertising task within the organisation when a number of the above criteria are applicable. That is, for reasons of time, or confidentiality, or scale of work, or lack of resources, or lack of a suitable local service, or when the job is so simple there is absolutely no need to call upon anyone else.

■ *When to use an advertising agency for some tasks:* an advertising agency may be of value when expertise is required, when the scale of the work in hand is beyond the scope of the advertiser, when time allows, and when the budget is sufficient.

The theory for a long time was that the services of an advertising agency came free and that the bulk of the agency's remuneration derived from the advertising media. In which case, it was prudent to use the service of an advertising agency. It cost the advertiser nothing and indeed saved money because otherwise the advertiser would have to bear the cost from the internal overhead. This is no longer the case, as we shall see later in the chapter.

Commonly, when advertisers use an agency it is for major and specific parts of the advertising programme only and not for the whole lot. For example, the agency itself would deal with:

■ general strategy development
■ producing overall concepts, themes, graphics or slogans
■ media planning and placement
■ production for the media advertisements so placed.

Typically, the advertiser would deal directly with:

■ print and literature production
■ exhibition stand construction
■ general product photography
■ direct mail.

These elements would not usually be covered by media commission and the advertiser would then have to pay the agency an extra handling charge.

So, a key decision for the advertiser is to specify the split in tasks between the agency and himself, and to make these allocations clear to all parties. The basis most popularly followed is the split between media-related and non-media-related activities.

When to use a media independent

In the case of the media independent, this provides a media

planning and buying service only, leaving the advertiser to provide for the other elements; that is creative work and production. Here the advertiser can follow one of three methods:

1. The media independent deals with the media, the advertiser does the creative work, in-house.
2. The creative work is done by a traditional advertising agency, which does everything it normally would do except buy media space.
3. The creative and production work is contracted out to a studio or design and creative group, working on a fee.

Many advertisers today follow a mixed method. There are three main advantages. First, it may save the advertiser money – by gaining a rebate off the media commission from the media independent and then keeping some of it. A typical illustration of this effect is: media commission 15 per cent, kept by media independent 4 per cent, given to advertising agency 8 per cent, retained as a saving by the client 3 per cent. The second benefit is that the media independent may provide the greater media expertise and the advertising agency the greater creative expertise. And the third advantage is where a very large advertiser retains a number of agencies for a wide portfolio of brands. One overall media buying shop, buying across the range, may provide greater media coherence than buying from agency to agency.

As against this, splitting the functions in the way described may be time consuming, complex and difficult, and may dilute control rather than improving it, by spreading decision making too widely. It may also demotivate the advertising agency. And it is only suitable for big enough products with big enough budgets.

A local retailer spending £200 in a week in a local newspaper would hardly be able to operate a media independent/advertising agency allocation. It just would not be practical.

When to use an advertising agency for more tasks

Some advertisers use an agency not just for media-related activities, but for other necessary communication activities. These could include direct mail, exhibitions, print and literature, telemarketing and market research.

The benefits of using an agency in such an overall manner are considerable:

■ it saves time
■ it makes for a more cohesive and integrated programme
■ it can save on overheads.

The agency may have considerable expertise in all these extra areas, and not just in media advertising. Many agencies do provide an extensive range of services, and are pleased to make them available.

However, one area where agencies do sometimes hesitate is that of public relations. Some agencies provide PR services, or run their own PR department, but many regard this as a difficult and overspecialised area to tackle. Some advertisers use a combined advertising/PR service, but many do not and prefer to keep them separated.

The key point in deciding how far to use an agency is that of money. Which route is the more economic?

The advertiser has to cost out the following two factors as precisely as possible:

1. Cost of the advertising agency: all fees, production charges and other costs.
2. Cost of in-house operation: cost of staff, overheads, operating expenses.

The final decision is cost driven. Although some advertisers do shy away somewhat from giving their advertising agency too much work, they prefer to spread the risk.

WHAT TO PAY

The advertiser is naturally keen to know what to pay suppliers, what not to pay suppliers and when to pay. Remunerations and charges are often the cause of considerable suspicion, disagreement and acrimony. Payments commonly fall into three categories:

1. commission based income (especially applicable to advertising agencies)
2. cost-plus based
3. fee based.

In reality, payments are usually a mix of all three.

Advertising agencies and commission

The traditional mode of payment was for a long period that of commission. The *media* remunerated the agency, not the *advertiser!* A recognised agency was and is allowed a commission of up to 15 per cent. But there are in practical terms three remuneration situations:

1. On smaller accounts, where the agency may ask for a fee on top of commission, to make up for low income.
2. On medium-sized accounts, where media commission is satisfactory to both parties, and provides the agency with a reasonable income base.
3. On larger accounts, where the client may require the agency to rebate part of the commission, if the agency's income seems unduly large.

By way of illustration:

■ *Situation one.* The client spends £10,000. The agency gets £1500 in media commission but has £4000 costs. It may ask for a fee of £2500 to make up the difference.

■ *Situation two.* The client spends £100,000. The agency earns £15,000 in commission, has £14,000 costs and a small profit of £1000. No arguments!

■ *Situation three.* The client spends £10 million. The agency in theory is due to receive £1.5 million in media commission. The agency costs are factored out and come to £1 million. A profit of £500,000 is judged to be excessive and the client calls for a 50:50 profit split – a rebate of £250,000.

What this means is that agency remuneration has become more complex than previously, and that the commission system no longer suffices in a large number of cases.

Cost-plus based charges

Many suppliers operate on a cost-plus basis. This is common for printers, direct mail houses, stand fitters, telemarketers, film production companies and a host of others.

By and large, cost-plus applies when the supplier actually produces a tangible and physical product or service and can calculate the base cost of production. Here the advertiser can check to find out, if possible, the mark-up or margin on prime cost. The supplier is naturally not always happy to indicate this. But the cost is relatively simple to evaluate.

Here, of course, the main question is to decide by how much the basic cost is to be marked up. There are often industry norms, as with printers. A reasonable margin is normally acceptable, but should be subject to open and clear negotiation.

Fees

Many agency–client arrangements are fee based, as are PR contracts or charges by those suppliers charging not so much for physical goods as for their time. Examples again are design and creative fees. Here there may arise a number of difficulties; for example:

■ there are no cost standards or averages for comparison
■ the fee is not necessarily related to the outcome.

Design Group A ask £25,000 to design a logotype and Design Group B asks for £2500. Is Design Group A a bunch of thieves? Or is Design Group B merely second-rate and not worth more?

The media commission system is a matter of mechanics. The fee system is – unfortunately, perhaps – more a matter of judgement.

Where a fee is asked, the advertiser should call for a justification. In practice, most fees are based on one or other of two approaches:

1. what the traffic will bear
2. staff time.

In the latter, staff time is calculated, an average hourly rate is levied for salaries, and an overhead factor is added.

The client is entitled to, and *must* receive, a full explanation.

Here, it is quite common for the client to ask for supplier time-sheets to be tendered on a monthly basis.

WHEN TO PAY

Usually, jobs of a one-off kind are paid on completion. Sometimes payments are requested on a staged basis, with a proportion paid on commission or halfway through.

With continuing advertising agency charging, the agency will charge:

■ monthly, for that month's media
■ on completion for production and other *ad hoc* jobs.

The client will ask for a reasonable period of credit: 30 days is the norm. Interestingly, the client may receive worse credit terms when buying media direct, and may sometimes be asked to pay up front when not known by those media. Agencies may be more liberal.

TYPE OF SUPPLIER

Advertisers need to look for specialist suppliers; that is, those most suitable to the job in hand. Suppliers tend not to be general, but specific. The advertiser requires a specific service for a specific task. Therefore, the advertiser must define what the task is and what the expertise must accordingly be. For advertising agencies there is a wide span of expertise. Agencies tend to specialise. For example:

■ recruitment agencies
■ business-to-business agencies
■ high-tech agencies
■ direct marketing agencies
■ specialists in travel and leisure
■ financial agencies
■ agencies with expertise in local government work.

The advertiser matches the profile of the agency with the profile of the project. For other suppliers, the fit must be with the *type of job*, such as:

Printers
Those suitable for long runs, or for small runs, or for display material, or printing on plastics. Printers vary extensively in expertise and technology offered.

TV film companies
Animation specialists, those with abilities to shoot on location, those good for large production values, those good for small.

Design groups
Those with expertise in the particular field required. Expertise
again varies widely. Some designers work best on brochures, some
on packaging, some on logotypes and corporate design.

Again, suppliers vary by size and location. Some advertisers are
comfortable with large suppliers. Some prefer smaller. Some have
no views on size.

Certainly, however, many advertisers prefer a supplier who can
offer *convenience*, who is local, or who anyway can provide quick
access.

And a key requirement is increasingly that of *service*. The
supplier must not only produce a product, at a reasonable price,
but do so speedily, easily and reliably. The advertiser does not want
aggravation. Service may perhaps count more than anything else.

HOW TO SELECT

Selection of the right business associate is critical. The advertiser
must approach this task in a professional way.

Identification

How does the advertiser identify a supplier? There are a variety of
means.

- Asking friends or colleagues in other companies.
- Contacting trade associations (many suppliers are in trade
  bodies that can be helpful).
- Checking through trade directories, or member lists.
- Asking other present suppliers: agencies will nominate
  printers, direct mail houses will nominate designers etc.
- Using a professional search method. Various consultancies exist
  to help select advertising agencies. They are useful, for expertise and general knowledge. But they can also be intrusive,
  expensive and impose their own views. Or try to sell their old
  friends.
- Running an advertisement. Advertising for suppliers can be hit
  or miss. The good ones may not reply.
- Reading the trade press. Here there is a problem with bias, or
  the fact that some suppliers are low profile.

Evaluation

The advertiser needs to draw up a profile or outline of the service sought:

■ how local, or national?
■ what expertise?
■ what size?
■ what service requirement?
■ what budget?

The list of candidate suppliers will be checked against these criteria. Three things might then be done:

1. The candidate will be asked to show specimens of similar work, and explain what sort of work has been done for other clients.
2. The candidate will be asked to specify the team or person who will work with the client. Those people will be closely scrutinised.
3. The candidate *may* then be asked to produce a proposal on how they would service the client or help solve the client's problem. This may be done informally, as discussion, or formally, as a detailed report. Sometimes, an advertising agency may be asked to show sample creative work in regard to the client's product. Agencies will often ask for a rejection fee, if creative work is requested.

Finally, the potential supplier will be asked for a cost specification or an estimate or quotation.

If in doubt, the advertiser will ask for trade references, or go to Companies House in London for the supplier's accounts and past history.

If the fit is comfortable, the terms acceptable and the idea sensible, the advertiser will proceed.

SUPPLIER CHECKLIST

■ What *kind* of supplier is needed?
■ What is the preferred location or area?
■ What expertise is needed:
  – technique?
  – experience?
■ What service back-up is necessary?
■ Is there a preferred *size* of supplier?
■ What should their track record and level of success be?
■ What other sorts of company should they be working for?
■ Is there any exclusivity required?
■ What should their job be precisely?
■ How large is the budget?
■ How is the supplier going to be remunerated?
■ Does the advertiser have a standard or a norm on the size and extent of this remuneration?
■ What credit terms are wanted?
■ How much time has the supplier got?
■ Who will the supplier report to?
■ Is the advertiser prepared to pay the supplier for a speculative presentation, or advance piece of work?
■ Which person or persons will the supplier allocate to the client?
■ How much time will they give?
■ How will they charge:
  – what type of charge?
  – how is this charge composed?

Further Reading

Some useful further reading is suggested below.

Broadbent, S and Jacobs, B (1984) (4th ed) *Spending Advertising Money*, Century Business Books.

Crimp, M (1989) *The Marketing Research Process*, Prentice-Hall International.

Davies, M. (1992) (4th ed) *The Effective Use of Advertising Media*, Century Business Books.

Hart, NA (1993) *Industrial Marketing Communications*, Kogan Page.

The Incorporated Society of British Advertisers (ISBA) also produces a useful range of handbook guides, listed below:

Choosing an Advertising Agency
Guide to Direct Mail
Guide to Outdoor Advertising
Guide to Business to Business Advertising
Guide to Buying Media Direct

Index